The aim of Zenith Books is to present the history of minority groups in the United States and their participation in the growth and development of the country. Through histories and biographies written by leading historians in collaboration with established writers for young people, Zenith Books will increase the awareness of minority group members of their own heritage and at the same time develop among all people an understanding and appreciation of that heritage.

Dr. JOHN HOPE FRANKLIN, Professor of History at the University of Chicago, has also taught at Brooklyn College, Fisk University, and Howard University. For the year 1962–1963, he was Pitt Professor of American History and Institutions at Cambridge University in England. He is the author of many books including *From Slavery to Freedom, The Militant South, Reconstruction After the Civil War,* and *The Emancipation Proclamation.*

SHELLEY UMANS is a specialist in reading instruction and is a member of the instructional staff of Teachers College, Columbia University. For more than ten years, she has been a consultant to many major urban school systems throughout the United States. She is the author of *New Trends in Reading Instruction* and *Designs for Reading Programs.*

CAROL F. DRISKO is Associate Editor of Scholastic Magazines. She was formerly School Program Coordinator for WQED-ETV in Pittsburgh, Pennsylvania.

DR. EDGAR A. TOPPIN is Professor of History at Virginia State College. He previously taught at the University of Akron. Dr. Toppin has published numerous articles for historical journals and is co-author of *Pioneers and Patriots,* another Zenith Book. He is a member of the Executive Council of the Association for the Study of Negro Life and History.

TRACY SUGARMAN graduated from the Syracuse University School of Fine Arts and studied at the Art School of the Brooklyn Museum. Among the books he has illustrated are *Feeling of Jazz* and *I Have A Dream.* He is also the author of *Stranger at the Gates.*

THE UNFINISHED MARCH

The Negro in The United States,
Reconstruction to World War I

CAROL F. DRISKO and
EDGAR A. TOPPIN, Ph.D.

Illustrated by Tracy Sugarman

ZENITH BOOKS
DOUBLEDAY & COMPANY, INC., GARDEN CITY, NEW YORK
1967

The Zenith Books edition, published simultaneously in hardbound and paperback volumes, is the first publication of *The Unfinished March*.

Zenith Books edition: 1967

CONTENTS

——◆——

Chapter 1

THE LIGHT OF FREEDOM

———◆———

To Negroes, the year 1865 seemed full of hope and promise. They were freedmen—"free at last, free at last!"

Those who had been slaves were set free from their plantation masters as the Union soldiers swept across the South. Other Negroes who were already freedmen had fought bravely in the Civil War; 38,000 of them had been killed in the fighting.

A long war had been fought to keep the United States one country and to free the Negro slaves. In the four years of the Civil War, 618,000 men, North and South, had died. In 1865 white Americans asked themselves: "What more does the Negro want? The war is over; now he's free."

The answer was not hard to figure out. The freedman wanted to try out his freedom. He wanted to see if he could move from place to place without asking permission. He wanted enough to eat, a place to live, a way to earn a living. He wanted land of his own to farm. He was eager for a chance to learn to read and write, and he especially wanted education for his children.

But the freedman was having a hard time fulfilling his wishes. He had no land, no mules, no tools, no money, and no way to borrow money from a bank.

The freedman was eager for a chance to learn
to read and write, and he especially wanted
education for his children.

Frederick Douglass, the chief Negro leader through the war years, said that the freedmen "were sent away empty handed, without money, without friends, without a foot of land to stand upon. Old and young, sick and well, they were turned loose to the open sky . . . to their enemies."

Even if the freedmens' former masters had wanted to help—and few did—they could not do much. The South had been ruined by war. Fields lay in waste, many cities were smoking ruins, homes were crumbling, grass grew in the roads, livestock had wandered away from the farms. The few factories the South had were leveled.

People—Negro and white—wandered in search of food and shelter. They lived on the outskirts of cities, in makeshift shanty towns without sanitation or heat. Disease swept across the region. Many thousands died.

What did freedom really mean to the Negro? The freedom to be sick, cold, hungry? To starve? As one freedman said, "We soon found out that freedom could make folks proud, but it didn't make 'em rich."

The U. S. Congress had set up the Freedmen's Bureau in 1865 to help the newly freed Negroes find homes and work. It provided food, clothing, fuel, and medical care.

But the Freedmen's Bureau could only skim the surface of the problem, for it had a short life of seven years. In that time, it set up forty hospitals and more than 4000 day, night, and industrial schools. These schools were attended by nearly a quarter of a million former slaves.

Half a million acres of land were distributed to 40,000 Negroes by the Bureau. Soon afterward, however, the Federal government pardoned the old landowners for supporting the Confederacy. Their land was returned to them, and the Negroes who had settled on it were driven off.

The Freedmen's Bureau set up special courts to settle disputes between freedmen and their former owners. The Bureau worked out fair contracts between freedmen and those who wanted to hire them, making sure that the Negroes were fairly treated and paid for their work.

The South had to be rebuilt—its cities, its farms, its factories, its schools. This work was known as *Reconstruction.*

A great debate was waged over who would lead Reconstruction and how it would be carried out. Should it be Congress, the President, or the South itself? Whoever led would have the most to say about what would be done.

Reconstruction had started long before the war was won—and so did the debate. President Abraham Lincoln started thinking about Reconstruction soon after the first shot of the Civil War was fired at Fort Sumter in 1861.

As Northern soldiers began to occupy parts of the South, the problem became more urgent. New governments had to be set up to take the place of the fallen Confederate governments.

By the end of 1863, President Lincoln began to set forth his plan for Reconstruction. This plan was based partly on his view of secession. He believed secession was unconstitutional and denied the right of any state to leave the Union. Thus, the eleven states of the South had never withdrawn from the Union.

The problem, according to the President, was how to restore as quickly as possible the old relationship be-

tween North and South. To Lincoln, the war had been
fought not by Southern states but by Southern citizens
who were misled by their leaders. They were now ready
to come back. He felt this attitude was the only way to
heal the awful scars of a war between brothers—and to
make Americans feel part of one nation again.

His plan offered a full pardon to all who would take
an oath of allegiance or loyalty to the national government. The only Southerners the President excluded were
men who had left civil and military posts with the Federal government to serve the South; members of the
Confederate government; Confederate Army officers
above the rank of colonel and Navy officers above the
rank of lieutenant.

In states where 10 percent of the citizens who had the
right to vote in 1860 took the oath, the state could
write a new state constitution, elect officials, and set up
a government.

Lincoln's plan left Reconstruction to the same men
who had fought against the Union. In addition, his plan
would have kept Negroes from taking part in Reconstruction, since few of them had the right to vote in
1860.

A number of the Radical Republicans in Congress,
such as Thaddeus Stevens of Pennsylvania and Charles
Sumner of Massachusetts, disagreed with Lincoln's plan.
First, they believed it was the job of Congress, not the
President, to work out Reconstruction plans. Second,
they believed the South had seceded from the Union
and committed treason, and therefore should be pun-
ished. The Southern states, in their view, were conquered
provinces that should not expect leniency. Third, these

Congressmen were Republicans who wanted to build up their party in the South. The quickest way to do this would be to gain the support of the new Negro voters. Finally, the Radical Republicans did not want the freedmen's future to be put back into the hands of the same people who had fought a war to preserve slavery.

The radical Congressmen favored a harsher plan of Reconstruction than Lincoln's. They would require 50 percent of the voters to take an oath of allegiance to the Union. This oath would not only declare *future* allegiance to the Union but also would require *past* loyalty. In other words, to take the oath honestly, a person would have to say he had opposed the Confederacy from its very beginning.

Lincoln thought the Congressional plan was too severe and refused to approve it. No one knows what Lincoln would finally have done about Reconstruction, since he was assassinated before his plan was completed.

Andrew Johnson, a staunch Union supporter, became President at Lincoln's death. Johnson came from the mountains of eastern Tennessee, a region of small, poor farms. Perhaps because of this, he was firmly and bitterly opposed to the rich Southern planters. He blamed them for dragging the South into secession and war to further their own interests. Although opposed to the planters, he had not been against slavery, having owned eight slaves himself. Johnson was a self-educated man, whose wife taught him to read after their marriage. Proud, stubborn, and short-tempered, he lacked the tact, patience, and self-control of Lincoln.

At first the Radicals thought Johnson would support their ideas on Reconstruction. In early talks with them, he sounded firm in his support of their plans. But he was only firm in his dislike of the rich planters.

Without waiting for Congress to meet, Johnson began putting his own brand of Reconstruction into practice. He preferred to call it "Restoration." Johnson's Restoration turned out to be even more lenient than Lincoln's Reconstruction. Troops were sent home rapidly, leaving only a few thousand behind in the South.

Johnson began granting pardons to Southerners who applied to him by letter or in person. By September 1865, he was granting about a hundred pardons a day. Pardoning became a big business, with many Southerners paying bribes to the proper government officials to get pardons. In two years Johnson granted 13,500 pardons. This meant that more and more ex-Confederates regained the right to vote. President Johnson was against giving freedmen the right to vote. He said it would give Negroes control and would "Africanize the [Southern] half of our country."

One state after another was quickly "restored" to the Union under Johnson's plan. The pardoned Confederates voted, set up governments, and elected men to office. In 1866, they elected to Congress the Vice-President of the Confederacy, Alexander H. Stephens, four Confederate generals, six Confederate Cabinet officers, and 58 Confederate Congressmen. They elected former rebels at the state and local level as governors, sheriffs, judges, and legislators. The newly elected Louisiana state lawmakers defiantly and proudly wore their gray Confederate uniforms to meetings of the legislature.

The same leaders whom the North had fought for four bitter and bloody years were back in power!

The Southern legislatures began to take bold steps. The South had not had free public schools before the war. Schools were set up—but not for Negro children. The South Carolina legislature vowed to "educate every white child" in the state.

Within a year after the war, many Southern legislatures passed laws affecting the life and work of Negroes. These laws were called "Black Codes." They gave the Negro a glimpse of what his future "place" might be if the South had its way. Under the codes:

• A Negro who quit a job before his contract was ended could be arrested.

• Negroes could be witnesses in court only if another Negro was involved in the case.

• Any Negro without a job could be arrested. If he could not pay a $50.00 fine, he could be hired out to any person who paid it.

Across the South, Negroes held mass meetings—more than a dozen in 1865 alone. They spoke out against the Black Codes and asked the President and Congress for protection.

The Radical Republicans in Congress were bitter. They said the former rebels were plotting new rebellions and putting Negroes back into slavery. They refused to seat the newly elected Senators and Representatives from the South.

The Radicals said the South was winning back what it had lost at Appomattox Courthouse (where the Confederate General Robert E. Lee surrendered to the Union General Ulysses S. Grant). They accused Johnson of losing the peace for the North.

Congress held hearings on Reconstruction. These were the first large-scale Congressional investigations in U.S. history.

Information was gathered on treatment of Negroes by white Southerners; on the need for the Freedmen's Bureau and for Federal troops in the South; on feelings of the South about the Union.

Congress learned that white hoodlums throughout the South were terrorizing Negroes and whites who associated with them.

Riots broke out against Negroes in New Orleans and Memphis. In both cities, the police joined in the attack. General Philip H. Sheridan, the Union leader, witnessed the New Orleans riots. He said they were not riots "but an absolute massacre by the police" with the full knowledge of the mayor.

These events led Congress to conclude that Reconstruction managed by the South had been a huge mistake. Congress decided to take action. If the Negro was not to be put back into chains, Reconstruction must be run by Congress and not by President Johnson.

An increasing number of Radical Republicans were elected to Congress in 1866. They had gained enough votes to push the laws needed for their plan through Congress.

Johnson stubbornly opposed the Congressional plan every step of the way. It became an open battle with both sides name-calling and making bitter accusations. At the bottom of this argument were honest and serious differences. Who should have more power—the President or Congress, the Federal or the state governments? The conflict led to the impeachment of Johnson by the

House of Representatives. He was then tried by the Senate but was found not guilty of the charges by one vote. He was not removed from office, but he lost the power to affect the course of Reconstruction—and Congress took over its leadership.

Radical Reconstruction rested on three important amendments passed by Congress and approved by three-fourths of the states in the early years of Reconstruction. These amendments were added to the Constitution and became the law of the land.

THE 13TH AMENDMENT said slavery shall not exist in the United States. It became a law in December, 1865.

THE 14TH AMENDMENT said all persons born in the United States are citizens, entitled to equal protection under law. This amendment was not approved until 1868.

THE 15TH AMENDMENT assured that any citizen's right to vote could not be denied him because of "race, color, or previous condition of servitude [slavery]." It became part of the Constitution in 1870.

Each amendment gave Congress the power to pass further laws, if needed, to make sure that the purposes of the amendments were carried out. Congress decided further laws were needed and passed the Reconstruction acts of 1867.

These laws said the South was to be divided into five military districts, each one under the command of a general of the Union Army. Negroes were to be given the right to vote and even whites who had been pardoned would have to take a strict oath in order to vote. The military commanders had the right to keep law and order. They also were given the task of calling conventions of eligible Negroes and whites to write new Constitutions and to set up new governments for the Southern states.

Thus, two years after the war's end, Reconstruction started all over again. Johnson's plan of Reconstruction was erased. Now Reconstruction was to be run by Congress. It looked as if the dream of freedom for the Negro might become a bright reality after all.

Chapter 2

FREEDOM WITHIN THEIR
GRASP

———◆———

What was Radical Reconstruction like? Who were the
"Reconstructors?" Who were the New South's leaders?
What happened after Congress passed the Reconstruc-
tion acts of 1867?

Constitutional Conventions were called in each Southern state. The delegates were Negroes, white Southerners, and men from the North. They wrote new Constitutions and made new laws to govern former slave
states.

The new laws, and the men who made them, were
hated by most white Southerners. They scornfully
called the men from the North *carpetbaggers*. (Many
carried their belongings in a kind of cloth suitcase with
a carpetlike covering.)

Southern whites who cooperated with Reconstruction
were nicknamed *scalawags*. Southerners were even more
bitter toward scalawags than carpetbaggers. They considered them good-for-nothing traitors who had be-
trayed their own people.

The former Confederates thought Reconstruction was
a plot to give the Negro a chance to seek revenge for
more than two hundred years of slavery. For years

planters had feared slave revolts. These fears lived on, and grew even greater after the Civil War.

Surprisingly, most Negroes were not bitter toward their old masters, though they had a right to be. The freedmen were willing to look ahead rather than to the past. Negroes in Mississippi, for example, asked Congress to give back the right to vote to white Mississippians as soon as possible.

A striking and revolutionary change was taking place in the Reconstruction South. Many Negroes voted for the first time in the elections of 1867–68. Out of 4,000,000 Negroes, about 700,000 qualified as voters (660,000 Southern whites also registered to vote).

Many of the new voters, both Negro and white, were unable to read or write. Since the South had very few free public schools before the war, the poor whites were illiterate. And it had been a crime to teach slaves to read and write in most Southern states. As a result, many former slaves and poor whites had no idea of what the complicated process of registering and voting involved. In this, they were no different from hundreds of thousands of European immigrants who were voting for the first time in cities of the North.

Negroes themselves spoke often about the new responsibilities of citizenship. They were the first to recognize their shortcomings. Beverly Nash, a former slave, was a member of the convention elected to draw up a new state constitution for South Carolina. He said:

"I believe, my friends and fellow citizens, we are not prepared for this suffrage [voting]. But we can learn. Give a man tools and let him commence to use them, and in time he will learn a trade. So it is with voting. We may not understand it at the start, but in time we shall learn to do our duty."

A number of talented leaders came from the ranks of Negro freedmen. A former slave, Blanche K. Bruce, was a U. S. Senator from Mississippi. P. B. S. Pinchback was the Lieutenant Governor of Louisiana. There were two Negro lieutenant governors of South Carolina. Negroes served as superintendents of schools, state treasurers, sheriffs, policemen, judges. A Negro was mayor of Natchez, Mississippi. From 1869 to 1877, two Negro Senators and 14 Negro Representatives served in the United States Congress.

Some of the Negro leaders had been born into families that were free before the war. Others were the sons of planters, who had sent them to the best colleges in the North, or to Canada or Europe to be educated.

Others were self-educated. One man who became speaker of the house in Mississippi and later a member of Congress, John Roy Lynch, received his education secondhand. While working in a photographer's studio, he would gaze out the window into a white classroom across the alley. He kept up with the class and mastered the subjects at long-distance!

Among the new Negro leaders was Henry MacNeal Turner. He was born free in South Carolina, but after his father's death he was hired out to a planter under conditions little better than slavery. At age 12 he refused to allow overseers to beat him, and at 15 he ran away. He learned to read and write, with the help of friendly whites, when possible, or by himself with a Bible and a hymnbook.

Elected to the first Reconstruction legislature of Georgia, he defended his right to hold office: ". . . I hold that I am a member of this body. Therefore, sir, I shall neither fawn nor cringe before any party, nor stoop to beg for my rights. . . . I am here to demand my rights . . ."

Another leader was Joseph Rainey of South Carolina, the first Negro elected to Congress. Born a slave, his freedom and that of his whole family had been purchased by their father with his earnings as a barber. During the war, rather than help build Confederate fortifications, Rainey fled to the West Indies.

The allies of the Negroes, the carpetbaggers, had gone South for varied reasons. Some went South to buy cotton lands, to build factories and railroads, to open businesses, to develop natural resources, such as coal, iron ore, and timber. Some of the carpetbaggers were former Union soldiers, who had liked the land and the climate of the South, and saw its many opportunities. Some stayed on at the end of the war, others returned later. Many came with the Freedmen's Bureau to set up schools and hospitals and to distribute food and medicine.

Of the scalawags, a few had been in favor of the Union all through the war. Others were poor white farmers who opposed the planter class. Some joined the new governments because they felt it was the most sensible way to set about rebuilding the South. Others were businessmen with Northern connections, who favored the economic policies of the Republican party.

Southerners charged the new governments of "Negro rule" and "carpetbag control." A check of the number of Negroes and whites elected to the state conventions which drew up the Radical Reconstruction constitutions shows:

	NEGRO	WHITE
Alabama	18	90
Arkansas	8	58
Florida	18	27
Georgia	33	137
Louisiana	49	49
Mississippi	16	84
North Carolina	15	118
South Carolina	76	48
Virginia	25	80
Texas	9	81

Only in South Carolina did Negroes have a majority of members in the convention. In one other state, Louisiana, they held 50 percent of the seats, by law. Carpetbaggers had a majority in only one state, Mississippi.

Under the Radical governments, the states provided new services to the public. By 1870 free schools for all children had been opened throughout the South. Public hospitals, asylums for the deaf and blind, and old-age homes were set up for the first time.

The new state governments rebuilt roads, bridges, and public buildings destroyed by the war. They tried to strengthen the economy of the South by building more railroads. Since the South had lagged far behind the North in railroads even before the war, the task after the war was that much bigger. The planters complained of rising taxes—and many refused to pay them. The state governments, unable to raise enough money for these projects, had to borrow huge sums. The states' debts mounted.

Money was often spent unwisely or dishonestly. State money might be paid out for railroad tracks that were never laid. Bribes were paid by railroad officials and other businessmen to state legislators to have laws passed that were favorable to them.

But it must be remembered that dishonesty in government and business was widespread in the 1870's. It was not confined to one section of the country, to one political party, or to one race. Financial scandals were uncovered among Congressmen and among high officials in President Ulysses S. Grant's administration.

A few years after the leaders of the Old South returned to power, a number of state officials were discovered dipping freely into state funds. Although they used waste and corruption as an argument against the Radical governments, the corruption did not end when they returned to power.

But Southerners' main objection to the Reconstruction governments was not their so called "corruption" but their attempt to make over the old Southern way of life.

Many white Southerners held on to their old beliefs about slavery. Former Confederates were not about to give up these ideas. The South was determined to rid itself of Radical Reconstruction by any means possible.

Southerners spoke of the "harsh" years of "Black Reconstruction" and said that the governments controlled by "niggers," carpetbaggers, and scalawags were wasteful and corrupt. They said there was no law and order.

It was necessary, they said, to bring "law and order" back to the South. As early as 1866—only one year after the war and one year before Radical Reconstruction began—defeated Confederates began to lay out their own brand of "law and order." They began to take the law into their own hands.

Six young men who had been officers in the Confederate Army formed a club in Pulaski, Tennessee. They used secret passwords and mysterious ceremonies. The "clubs" spread. They chose their name, Ku Klux, from a Greek word, *kyklos,* meaning circle. Later the word *Klan* (clan), meaning group, was added. Wearing robes and hoods made from bedsheets and pillowcases, they paraded through towns at night on horses draped in sheets. These ghostly figures paid visits to Negroes to frighten them. Years later a former slave recalled, "They wore long sheets and covered the hosses with sheets so you couldn't recognize 'em. Men you thought was your friend was Ku Kluxes, and you'd deal with 'em in stores in the daytime, and at night they'd come to your house and kill you."

The Klan claimed it was a patriotic organization dedicated to defending women and children, but its real purpose was to prevent Negroes from voting. The Klan and other such groups worked to put state and local governments back into the hands of Southern white people. They called this bringing back "home rule." The Klan helped bring home rule back to Virginia, North Carolina, and Georgia as early as 1870.

The Klan kept "Dead Books." In them were listed the names of Negroes and their white allies. They were

Many Klansmen continued to ride at night in their own small bands.

marked men. Klansmen marched through some towns carrying empty coffins. On them were marked the names of local Reconstruction leaders.

In 1869, the head of the Klan himself grew embarrassed and disgusted at the open terror and tried to bring an end to the organization. Congress and some states passed laws that made such terrorism a crime. The Klan only became more secret. Many Klansmen continued to ride at night in their own small bands. The Klan never died completely. From time to time Klan groups sprang up again, to keep freedmen from being really free.

Chapter 3

A BRIGHT DREAM VANISHES

———◆———

Reconstruction came to an end gradually. Many Southerners refused to obey the laws of Reconstruction. The
North grew tired of forcing them to obey these laws.

Reconstruction ended without the Negro's getting
land, tools, or training for jobs. Without them he could
not be truly free.

A few Northern Radicals understood the freedmen's
needs for land and training to make their dream of freedom come true. But these political leaders were rare
and few people agreed with them or gave them support.

One such politician was the Senator from Massachusetts, Charles Sumner. During Reconstruction, Sumner
worked to have "public schools open to all without distinction of race or color." He tried to have the Senate
provide homes for all freedmen.

Another man was Thaddeus Stevens, a Representative from Pennsylvania who has been called the "Archi-
tect of Radical Reconstruction." Many of his ideas were
carried out during Reconstruction. Stevens wanted to
give each adult freedman "forty acres and a mule." He
believed the freedmen had earned their right to the
land by centuries of toil. When the House of Representa-

tives voted against this plan, Stevens rose up and said to its members:

"In my youth, in my manhood, in my old age, I had fondly dreamed" that we could change our ways of living and working to get rid of every trace of "human oppression and inequality of rights . . . This bright dream has vanished."

He died—a disappointed man—in 1868. Reconstruction would be dead in nine years. Home rule would be restored and white Southerners would control the governments.

By 1870, home rule was brought back in four states, with the help of the Klan—Tennessee, Virginia, North Carolina, and Georgia.

By 1874, Alabama, Arkansas, and Texas returned to home rule. In 1875, Mississippi followed, leaving only South Carolina, Florida, and Louisiana with Reconstruction governments.

In that year, a law to protect the rights of Negroes in public places came before Congress. James T. Rapier, a Negro Congressman, spoke eloquently in favor of the law. He pointed out that there was "not an inn between Washington and Montgomery, a distance of more than a thousand miles, that will accommodate me to a bed or a meal . . . Sir, I submit that I am degraded as long as I am denied the public privileges common to other men."

Congress passed the Civil Rights Act of 1875. It guaranteed Negroes equal rights to service at inns, theaters, on trains, boats, and in other public places. But the law made little difference in the lives of the Negroes, since it was not being enforced any place in

"In my youth, in my manhood, in my old age, I had dreamed we could get rid of every trace of human oppression and inequality of rights."

the South or the North. In 1883, the Supreme Court of the United States ruled that the law went against the Constitution. This decision along with others made by the Court whittled away the rights of Negroes and gave the go-ahead signal for Southern states to segregate.

From the 1870's on, various laws were passed to get around the 13th, 14th, and 15th Amendments. Open and secret methods were used to take away the Negro's vote. By depriving freedmen of the vote, former Confederates were able to put an end to Reconstruction governments.

In South Carolina, the Democrats drew up a "campaign plan" for the presidential election of 1876. Rule number 12 of the plan said:

"Every Democrat must feel honor bound to control the vote of at least one Negro by intimidation [threats], purchase, keeping him away [from the voting place], or as each individual may determine how he may best accomplish it."

In Mississippi during the elections:

• Voting booths were hidden in secret places. Hours of voting were set at odd times, such as before 7 A.M. or long after nightfall. The places and times of voting were suddenly changed—and only white voters were told of the changes.

• Cannons were trained on voting places. Cavalrymen from Alabama—which was under home rule—were brought in. They guarded roads leading from Negro districts to the polls and halted Negroes going to vote.

• Many white men agreed not to hire Negroes who voted for the Reconstruction party.

Voting cost many Negroes their homes and jobs—and often their lives.

The Reconstruction governor of Mississippi had begged President Grant to protect Negroes from violence during the elections. Grant's Attorney General replied: "The people are tired of these annual autumnal [election] outbreaks in the South." Mississippi returned to home rule in 1875.

In many Southern states open fighting went on all through the presidential election of 1876.

This election was very important for the Negroes in the South. It has gone down in history as a most unusual one, since the presidential candidate who won most of the popular votes lost the election.

This is possible because the U. S. President is elected by a count of the electoral votes of each state. Each state has as many electoral votes as it has Senators and Representatives in Congress. Under the electoral system whoever wins the most popular votes in any one state receives *all* the electoral votes of that state. Suppose 82,000 votes out of a total vote of 162,000 go to one candidate and 80,000 to the other. The candidate winning 82,000 votes wins all the state's electoral votes. The losing candidate—who really won nearly half of the popular votes—gets none of the electoral votes.

The election of 1876 was hard-fought and the vote was close. Both candidates claimed victory. The Democratic candidate, Samuel J. Tilden, had 4,284,757 popular votes to 4,033,950 for Rutherford B. Hayes, the Republican candidate.

Tilden had been Governor of New York and a crusader against crime and corruption. Hayes had been a Civil War general and a reform Governor of Ohio. Both men ran on a platform promising reforms. The 1870's had been marked by graft and dishonesty in government and business—both North and South.

On Wednesday, November 8, 1876, the day after the election, the early morning New York *Tribune* carried a banner headline: TILDEN ELECTED. Tilden had 184 electoral votes—only one short of the number he needed to be elected. Hayes had only 165 electoral votes. Tilden's supporters were certain he would pick up the one extra electoral vote.

Twenty electoral votes were being claimed by both candidates. The votes were from Oregon and the three Southern states that still had Reconstruction governments—South Carolina, Florida, and Louisiana. If the electoral votes of these states were counted in the column of Hayes, then he would be declared President.

Both parties had perhaps been guilty of cheating in counting the vote in these states. Two sets of returns had been sent in with both parties claiming victory. The dispute between the Republicans and Democrats went on from Election Day in November 1876 until March 1877, when the new President was to be inaugurated. No one could agree who had been elected President.

Many people feared that a civil war might start again if the election was not settled and a President decided upon. Veterans groups from 15 states were prepared to march on Washington, D.C., to make sure that

New-York Tribune.

NOVEMBER 8, 1876.

TILDEN ELECTED.

HIS ELECTORAL MAJORITY OVER 200
HAYES AND WHEELER HAVE ABOUT 150 ELECTORAL VOTES—THE U. S. SENATE WILL HAVE A REDUCED REPUBLICAN MAJORITY—THE HOUSE IS CLOSE, WITH A PROBABLE SMALL DEMOCRATIC MAJORITY.

Tilden and Hendricks are undoubtedly elected by a fair majority of the Electoral College. They have probably carried the "solid South" with the possible exception of South Carolina and Louisiana, have carried New-York by from 25,000 to 30,000 majority, Connecticut by about 1,500 majority, and New-Jersey by a reduced majority. They have carried Indiana by 10,000 majority. Their total vote in the Electoral College is likely to exceed 200. Hayes and Wheeler have carried all the New-England States except Connecticut, Pennsylvania, and all the Western States except Missouri. Their vote in the Electoral College will not fall much below 150.

The Republicans retain control of the United States Senate, but their majority, which is now 15, will certainly be reduced to 10, and possibly to 6. The House of Representatives is in doubt. The news thus far received makes it apparently Democratic by 18 majority, but the returns are so incomplete that later information may increase this or give it to the Republicans by a very small majority.

New-York has been carried by Tilden by about 30,000 majority. His majority in New-York City is 53,000 and in Kings County about 15,000. The Congressional delegation is substantially unchanged with a possible Republican gain of one or two. Full particulars of the vote in New-York will be found under the head of that State.

Returns from South Carolina, Louisiana, Florida, and Wisconsin are inconclusive, and no news whatever has been received from the Pacific States.

Tilden was inaugurated. Members of Congress started carrying arms. Many doubted the country would again choose a President peacefully. As the weeks went by, both sides threatened to inaugurate their own candidate.

Northern and Southern businessmen were tired of the quarrel and of the "Negro problem." Northern industrialists could not start new businesses and industries in the South until it settled down and grew peaceful. They also wanted men and women who would work hard for little pay.

Out of these hopes and fears grew the Compromise of 1877. This national bargain between conservative Northern Republicans and Southern Democrats in Congress dealt the final blow to Radical Reconstruction. The businessmen decided to support the candidate who would let the men of the old South regain control over the freedmen. This would give the businessmen the labor force they wanted.

Congress named an Electoral Commission in January 1877 to decide the disputed cases in the election. It met for a whole month—and decided for Hayes.

In the meantime, Hayes supporters had come to an agreement with certain important Southern Democrats in behind-the-scenes meetings. Hayes told the managing editor of the influential New Orleans *Times* "that carpetbag governments had not been successful; that the complaints of the Southern people were just in this matter; that he should require absolute justice and fair play to the Negro, but that he was convinced this could be got best and most surely by trusting the honorable and influential Southern whites."

In exchange for the electoral votes of South Carolina, Florida, and Louisiana, Hayes agreed to pull out the small number of Federal troops remaining in the South.

The South needed and wanted economic help, and Hayes agreed to have Congress vote funds to help the South build more miles of much needed railroads, to clear the harbors of Savannah, Mobile, and New Orleans, to rebuild canals, and to raise river levees. The South was also promised its share of Federal jobs.

In return for these favors, leaders of the Democratic party in South Carolina, Florida, and Louisiana agreed to swing their states' votes to Rutherford B. Hayes. The state boards that reviewed the election returns made a recount and gave the victory to Hayes. The final electoral count was: Hayes—185; Tilden—184.

On Friday, March 2, 1877, Congress declared Hayes President-elect, and he was inaugurated the following Monday, March 5. In April, Federal troops withdrew from South Carolina and Louisiana. The remaining "Black and Tan" governments fell and home rule returned.

No longer was there any power in the South to protect the Negro and to make sure he would be allowed to vote. The U. S. Army no longer stood guard during elections. Congress voted down bills calling for other Federal supervisors to watch over elections.

But Negroes were still voting, in spite of terror and violence. Some Negroes still served in the legislatures of North and South Carolina, Tennessee, and Mississippi. Many Negroes used the same hotels, inns, theaters, restaurants, waiting rooms, and railroad cars that whites did. For at least 20 years there was a seesawing back and forth. The future of the freedman was not yet settled.

The bargain of 1877 marked the beginning of an understanding between conservative Republicans and Southern Democrats. The two groups often joined together to vote against laws that might change the lives of Negroes for the better.

From the Civil War on, the Negro had thought of the Republican party as his party. It was the party of Abraham Lincoln, who had issued the Emancipation Proclamation. The Republican party was also the party of Stevens and Sumner, two leaders of Radical Reconstruction who had fought for Negro rights.

Southern whites looked upon things differently. To them—despite the bargain of 1877—the Republican party was responsible for the "evil days" that had fallen upon the South. They turned to the Democratic party, which in the South became the "White Man's Party."

For a short time the Republican party had looked to Negro votes as a way to stay in power in the South. They hoped to build up their party in the South by adding Negro voters. Then the Republicans began to lose interest in the Negro. Republican politicians and businessmen became more and more eager to heal the rift between North and South. They hoped to pick up support among the white voters of the South. Their votes would replace the Negro vote.

The Negro found he was no longer needed by the Republican party after the Compromise of 1877. One Negro newspaper editor wrote, "The Negroes felt that the party of Lincoln had deserted them." Worse still, they felt they had no other party to join.

Certainly the Democratic party in the South was "for whites only." It might welcome Negro votes, but it would do nothing to further their interests.

President Hayes started the "hands off" policy for the South. Leave the South alone, he believed, and it would solve its Negro "problem" best.

The President made a good-will tour of the South in 1877. In Atlanta, he told a group of Negroes that their rights and interests were safer in the hands of Southern white men than in the care of the Federal government.

However, the Negroes of the South had learned to have little faith in the Southern white man.

Chapter 4

FARMERS WITHOUT LAND

———◆———

After the Civil War, the freedmen did not receive the "forty acres and a mule" they hoped for. With this, they would have become landowners and independent farmers. Instead, most old Confederate plantations were returned to their former owners.

The freedmen found themselves drifting into a new form of slavery. It was called the *sharecropping system,* and it has lasted to the present day in some parts of the country.

A farmer or a planter with property allowed a landless man to farm a few acres. The landless man was called a "sharecropper," or a "cropper." The planter often loaned the cropper seed and tools, too. In exchange the cropper was to give the planter a share of the crop, usually the bigger share. A tenant was another kind of farmer without land. He paid rent, either in cash or work, for his few acres.

To get food and supplies—and sometimes even seed for planting—the cropper or tenant farmer promised to deliver part of his crop to the storekeeper. He usually made this promise long before he had even put the seed in the ground, and if his crop failed, he went into debt. Often the farmer tried to pay off what he owed the storekeeper. In many cases this would never be possible, because some storekeepers cheated in their book-keeping to make sure that the poor farmer was never free of debt.

Whole families often had to hire themselves out as cotton pickers to earn enough to live. From little children to grandmothers, they worked in the fields from sunrise to sunset. For this they earned a few cents a day. The freed Negroes who worked in the cotton fields lived little better than they had as slaves, and by 1900, three-fourths of the Negro farmers were croppers or tenants.

Another form of slavery that grew up in the "New" South was the "convict lease system." Men were put in prison for very small offenses. Sometimes they were jailed only if someone said they did something wrong.

Stealing a pig in Mississippi could get a man a long prison sentence. This law was called the "Mississippi Pig Law." It called for five years in jail for stealing a pig, a cow, or any property worth more than $10.

Once a man was in prison, he could be rented or loaned out as a laborer. Often he worked on roads or railroads. Dozens of prisoners were chained together by one leg or around the waist in what were called "chain gangs."

Before the war, Negroes had provided the South with most of its skilled workmen. Five out of every six skilled workers were Negroes. They had served as mechanics, carpenters, barbers, blacksmiths, bricklayers. In the years after the war, white workers began to squeeze Negro workers out of these jobs. Laws were passed requiring licenses for skilled jobs, and few Negroes were given the licenses they needed. By 1900, only five out of every hundred of the South's skilled workers were Negroes.

New industries grew up in the South—cotton mills, steel mills, mining. But most skilled jobs in them were open to whites only, and Negroes were barred even from moving into the new towns that grew up around the cotton mills.

These mill towns were filthy, the houses rickety, and the mill workers poorly paid. Cotton mill workers worked for seventy hours a week. Children earned about 10 or 12 cents a day. Grownups earned 40 to 50 cents.

Being white was the only thing that made these "poor whites" feel better than Negroes. White mill owners encouraged them to feel this way. It made them forget the low pay and the dirty mill town. And it kept Negro and white workers from getting together to help one another.

Labor unions were begun in several cities. However, Negroes were not allowed to join. Not being union members, Negroes were kept out of the training programs for many skilled jobs. They ended up being hired for the lowest-paid and dirtiest jobs, the ones no one else would do. Very often factory and mine owners hired Negroes as "strike breakers," and brought them in to work in place of white workers who were out on strike. This increased the bad feelings between white and Negro workers. From 1882 to 1900, there were 50 strikes by white workers protesting the hiring of Negroes.

As a result of despair and hard conditions, Negroes fled the South. In 1879 alone more than 40,000 left.

In the years after the Civil War, over 5000 Negroes rode the Western trails, herding millions of cattle.

They went to Kansas and other frontier states, looking for a better, safer life.

Some Negroes worked on the Western ranges as cowboys. In the years after the Civil War, over 5000 rode the Western trails, herding millions of cattle. They rode to Abilene, Dodge City, Cheyenne, Deadwood, Fort Laramie, and points west.

They made the long cattle drives as top cow hands, as ordinary cowboys, as cooks, and as wranglers. Some became skilled and famous. To others, it was just a day's work. A trail crew of eight cowboys usually had three Negroes and one Mexican. Most often the cook and the wrangler—the man who took care of the horses —were Negroes.

But even as cowboys, Negroes faced some barriers. One cowboy, who had worked for twenty years as a rider, roper, and cook on a huge ranch, said, "If it weren't for my old black face, I'd have been boss of one of these divisions long ago." A white cowboy who rode with him agreed, "He no doubt would have."

BRONCO SAM rode the Chisholm and Western Trails through what is now Texas, Oklahoma, Kansas, Nebraska, and South Dakota. He was known as a "buckeroo [who] wasn't afraid of anything and could ride them all."

"THORNT" BIGGS was said to be the best top hand in Wyoming. He helped make a fortune for his boss, Ora Haley, owner of the Two Bar brand. He taught hundreds of young men about the range cattle business.

JIM SIMPSON worked for the Flying E Ranch in Wyoming. He was known as "the best roper on the range." When he became too old and too heavy to ride well, he became a cowboy-cook and drove the chuck wagon over the trails. He got a reputation for being as good a cook as he had been a roper. In winter he played the fiddle for ranch house dances. He also became a friend, teacher, and adviser to the younger cowboys.

BOB LEMMONS had the job of catching wild horses, or mustangs. The men who did this were called *mustangers*. It was hard work, which took great skill and patience. Mustangers often had to trail the wild horses for days, sometimes weeks.

BILL PICKETT was a cowboy for the 101 Ranch and a star performer in their rodeo. This show traveled all over the U.S. and to many parts of the world, performing before kings and queens of Europe.

He became a top "bulldogger." In fact, he was the inventor of "bulldogging," called steer wrestling today. One eyewitness described how Bill bulldogged:

"He'd grab a horn in each hand and twist them until the steer's nose came up. Then he'd reach in and grab the steer's upper lip with his strong white teeth, throw up his hands to show he wasn't holding any more, and fall to one side of the steer, dragging along beside him until the animal went down."

Other performers in the world-famous 101 Rodeo were Tom Mix and Will Rogers.

Negro soldiers also served in the U. S. Army in the West. In 1866 Congress set up two Negro infantry regiments and two Negro cavalry regiments. The four Negro units were the 24th and 25th Infantry and the 9th and the 10th Cavalry. For thirty years after the Civil War, these units served on the U.S. frontier. They served from Mexico to Montana. They fought Comanches, Apaches, and Sioux, and they kept peace between cattlemen and farmers. They also tracked down outlaws. These same brave units later served gallantly in the Spanish-American War.

The despair and hard conditions of Negro life led not only to the move west. They also had another result—they reawakened an interest in spirituals, work songs, and folk blues. These songs told of the long years of Negro slavery in the United States. They had helped the Negro bear the heavy burden of his hard life in slavery.

Yet this music had been neglected and nearly lost. After the Civil War and the freeing of the slaves, many Negroes believed there were no longer any reasons to sing "sorrow songs," as spirituals were called by W. E. B. Du Bois, the historian, writer, and civil rights leader. Many Negroes wanted to forget the years of slavery. They were reminded of slavery every time they heard such spirituals as:

> "Nobody knows the trouble I've seen.
> Nobody knows but Jesus . . ."

The freedmen didn't realize that they hadn't left their sorrows behind. Unfortunately more troubles lay ahead. The Negroes had not yet laid down their heavy burdens. There would still be reasons to sing "sorrow songs."

This great body of folk music "remembered" Africa. In Africa, songs were used to express many different kinds of feelings and to teach young people the history

Men sang while they worked. The songs set the pace of the work and made it go more easily.

and customs of the tribes. Men and women sang while they worked. The songs set the pace of the work and made it go more easily. Slave owners in America realized the Negroes were used to working in groups and they worked harder and faster when they sang together. So the slaves were allowed to go on singing. In time the singers blended the work songs with religious music they heard white Southerners sing at revival meetings, and the spiritual, an entirely new kind of song, grew out of the mixture.

A few historians and musicians realized that the music of the slaves was important to save. The Freedmen's Bureau set about collecting the work songs and religious spirituals of the Negroes of the Port Royal Islands off the coast of South Carolina. The Bureau published *Slave Songs of the United States* in 1867. This saved a large body of music that might have been lost forever.

But it was not until 1871 that the music of the slaves was really saved for future generations. Spirituals were given a new lease on life by a group of nine young singers on tour. They introduced Negro spirituals to the country and to the world.

Seven of the singers had been slaves. All were students at Fisk University in Nashville, Tennessee, and their group was called the Fisk University Jubilee Singers. George L. White, the treasurer of Fisk, was also the music teacher. He decided to take the nine singers on a tour of the North to raise money for their school. At first the Fisk singers performed only songs like "Annie Laurie" and "Home, Sweet Home." Audiences listened and clapped politely, but they were bored with those familiar songs. Halls were half-empty and little money came in. Then, at Oberlin, Ohio, came the turning-point. The tired, discouraged singers began this song:

> "My Lord, He calls me,
> He calls me by the thunder!
> The trumpet sounds within-a my soul
> I ain't got long to stay here.
> Steal away, steal away,
> Steal away to Jesus . . ."

No one in the audience was tired or bored. They begged to hear more of these sad songs that were so new to them. The Fisk singers proudly sang out the songs of their past, and soon became famous throughout the United States and Europe.

Another type of music that the former slaves sang to express their feelings about their lives was the blues. Spirituals and work songs were sung by groups, but the blues were sung solo. A blues singer "talked" about poverty, loneliness, wandering, love troubles, losing a job, homesickness, sadness, brushes with the police. Along with the work songs and spirituals, the blues told of the Negroes' troubles during nearly three hundred years of slavery and the long road that followed.

Chapter 5

"WHITE MAN'S BURDEN"

———◆———

Certain ideas were becoming popular in the U.S. and the rest of the world at the end of the 1800's. They were ideas about differences among the races, which stated openly that some races were superior to others.

Ideas of superiority and inferiority based on race are called *racism.* Not only were some races considered superior to others, but certain groups within one race were believed to have better traits than others. Northern Europeans were considered "better" than people from Middle, Eastern, and Southern Europe.

Racism gave men an excuse to take advantage of other men, and it went hand in hand with other popular ideas of the day.

One of these ideas resulted from the misuse of new scientific theories about living things and their development over thousands of years. The twisted popular idea was commonly referred to as the "survival of the fittest." The belief was that through the centuries only the strongest, brightest, fittest animals survived the competition for food, shelter, and living space with other animals. This competition for survival was supposed to apply to man, the "highest" animal, as well.

These theories were used by the rich and the powerful to explain their huge fortunes. If others had this

strength, they said, they, too, would have been successful. The men who owned mines and factories did not
feel guilty in having people work long hours for low
wages. It was proper for "inferior" people who hadn't
survived as successfully as they to do the dirty work in
factories and mines!

These ideas of superior and inferior people were not
really new. Such false ideas go far back in history. But
in the late 1800's and early 1900's the ideas were dressed
in new clothes. Men updated the ideas and put them
into "scientific" language. The "science" justified the
U.S. government's "hands off" attitude on the question
of separation of the races.

After all, if people were naturally inferior, there was
nothing to be done about it. Superior people would
not want to associate with them. And no laws could
change their feelings of superiority.

A famous professor of political and social science at
Yale University, William Graham Sumner, put this idea
into often-quoted words: "Stateways cannot change
folkways." What he meant was that the laws or ways of
states cannot change the actions and ways of people.
This is similar to the arguments used in the 1896 decision of the Supreme Court, which ruled that separate
could be equal.

Popular magazines, newspapers, and books of the
time downgraded the Negro. He was portrayed as lazy,
thievish, and foolish—in fact, as everything that was bad
or unpleasant.

Magazines in the North that had once been anti-
slavery now printed articles expressing these ideas of
racism in a weaker form.

At the same time, books, plays, and magazines fostered a pleasant and romantic image of Southern life, especially in slavery times. There grew up in the North a sympathy for the "Old South." The plays and novels told sentimental tales about the South's "Lost Cause"— the Civil War.

The idea of large plantations where wealthy, charming people lived gracious lives surrounded by beautiful things appealed to many Northerners. Little did it matter that these pictures were not truthful. They described life as it was lived on very few of the plantations. The pictures completely ignored the fact that life in the Old South was based largely on the slavery and suffering of other men. The false story spread that Negroes were really happy, well cared for, and protected as slaves.

One popular novel, *The Clansman,* painted a romantic picture of the "heroic" Ku Klux Klan. It was made into a play which was said to have helped stir up prejudice during the Atlanta riots of 1906. In 1915, it was made into a silent motion picture called *Birth of a Nation.*

Racism could be seen in the writings of scholars. Historians, sociologists, and anthropologists wrote articles with titles such as, *'The Negro a Beast' or 'In the Image of God'; The Negro, A Menace to American Civilization.*

While the U.S. was busy fixing the place of the Negro in society—chaining him to the lowest rungs on the ladder—the nations of Europe were busy carving up Africa among themselves.

The same racist ideas that seemed to justify keeping the Negro down in the U.S. gave powerful nations the feeling that it was all right for them to acquire colonies in parts of the world where colored peoples lived.

This movement is known as *imperialism* (building empires) or *colonialism* (collecting colonies).

The riches of Asia and Africa—the minerals, the products of farm and forest, and the labor of the people— were used to enrich the traders, merchants, and manufacturers of Europe. Tea, coffee, sugar, tin, rubber, spices, and oil found their way to the homes and factories of Europe and America.

Imperialism was not new. It was as old as Rome— and older. Spain and Portugal had sent out fleets and armies, starting in the 1400's. They built vast empires. Spain had plundered the southern part of the New World and had sent home all the "gold of the Indies." In parts of New Spain, the native peoples, the Indians, were nearly wiped out. Other nations, Britain, France, the Netherlands, joined the "Race for Empire."

By the late 1800's, nations which had not been colonial powers before—Germany, Italy, Belgium, Japan, Russia —joined the race for new lands. The race quickened at this time mainly because of the rise of factories and machine-made goods. Europe needed raw materials for her factories and new markets for her manufactured goods.

The industrial nations had new instruments of warfare which the non-industrial nations of Africa, Asia, and South America did not have. With repeating rifles and machine guns it was easy to subdue or take over people armed with bows and arrows—and keep them subdued.

People at home liked the idea of having an empire.

They were proud of their nation's far-flung possessions. They were proud of the daring men who subdued, ruled, and extracted wealth from the colonies.

More theories grew up to justify imperialism. Some people were taken in by their own justifications. Many Europeans had the notion that they had a mission to bring civilization and Christianity to the "poor ignorant natives" of Africa, Asia, and the Americas.

At first the U.S. was not involved in these adventures. The U.S. had started out a colony of Britain. Our nation prided itself in its democratic traditions and sympathized with other colonial peoples. The American Revolution inspired many colonies in Latin America to seek their independence. Later the story of our revolution inspired Asian and African nationalist leaders.

For much of the 1800's, the U.S. had been involved with problems at home. There was the whole West to conquer. American historians wrote about the "Manifest Destiny" of the United States to move westward and settle the continent from coast to coast. This movement to the west satisfied for a time the urge of land-hungry Americans. The U. S. West was a substitute for overseas adventures. In the course of moving to the new lands, the settlers pushed aside the native Americans, the Indians. And a war was fought with Mexico which added much of the Southwest to the nation. Later, the country was faced with a Civil War. After the war, much building and rebuilding of railroads and factories was taking place.

However, toward the end of the nineteenth century, the U.S. became interested in what was happening outside its own borders. When it looked beyond, the U.S.

saw the race for an empire among the European nations. Not all Americans found this race attractive, but many who were in power did. They had developed a taste for an empire.

The U.S. had a taste of imperial adventure in 1893. In that year, U.S. businessmen gave support to a revolution in Hawaii. Then a U.S. diplomat in the islands stepped in to "protect American lives and property." He requested the aid of the U. S. Marines. The successful rebels demanded annexation by the U.S., but some Americans protested this, saying it was against the wishes of the people of Hawaii. Congress refused to annex Hawaii and an independent republic was set up. Later, in 1898, the nation felt differently. During the excitement of the Spanish-American War, Hawaii was added as a U.S. territory by an overwhelming vote of Congress.

The Spanish-American War marked a turning point for the United States. The nation entered the war, our leaders said, to help free the Cubans. When the U.S. emerged from the war, she was an imperial power with "dominion over palm and pine."

The war began in Cuba in 1898. Cuba and Puerto Rico, two Caribbean islands, were all that were left of the once powerful Spanish-American Empire. Between 1868 and 1878, there were uprisings on the islands against Spanish rule. In 1895 another revolt broke out. Land and factories owned by many Americans were damaged.

As the revolt grew, sensational stories appeared daily in U.S. newspapers giving details about Spanish tortures in Cuba. The stories excited the American public

and whipped up a spirit of war. President William Mc-
Kinley was not eager to go to war, but public opinion
was for it as were many men in the government. The
President was pushed into war by a series of events.

One of the most spectacular was the mysterious sink-
ing of the U.S. battleship, *Maine,* in Havana harbor.
The U.S. had sent the battleship *Maine* to Cuba in January 1898. The ship was to protect American lives and
property in Cuba. It also showed Spain that the U.S.
would take action, if necessary, to help Cubans. On
February 15, 1898, the *Maine* was blown up and more
than 250 men were killed. (Twenty of these men were
Negroes.) No one knows to this day what really caused
the explosion.

People in the U.S. jumped to the conclusion that
Spain had sunk the ship.

"Remember the Maine!" became a battle cry and
Americans demanded war. Spain even gave in to most
U.S. demands about Cuba. Despite Spain's wish to
avoid war, the President asked Congress to intervene in
Cuba. Congress voted to use U.S. land and sea forces
to win the full independence of Cuba.

The nation, North and South, responded to the drums
of war. It further helped reunite the two sections. They
had a war to win together. Senator Ben Tillman of
South Carolina recited this jingle:

"Populists, Democrats, Republicans are we,
    But we are all Americans to make Cuba free."

The first battle of the war begun over Cuba was fought
halfway round the world in the Philippines. Admiral

George Dewey, commander of the far eastern fleet of the United States Navy, had been alerted by the Assistant Secretary of the Navy, Theodore Roosevelt, of the possibility of war between the U.S. and Spain. As soon as war was certain, Dewey, who had been in Hong Kong at the time, sailed immediately for Manila Bay in the Philippines where he destroyed the Spanish fleet.

The U.S. had supplied arms to Filipino revolutionists, and later U.S. troops landed. The Spanish forces surrendered, but Filipinos were to continue fighting the American forces who refused them their independence.

More than two months after war was declared, the Atlantic fleet, a force of 17,000 men, poorly trained and poorly equipped, landed on the island of Cuba. The food was bad and the army did not have proper hospital or sanitary facilities. Hundreds died, not from the wounds of battle, but from malaria, yellow fever, typhoid, and dysentery.

Among the first troops to arrive were 600 Negro soldiers of the 24th Infantry. They were followed by the Negro 10th Cavalry. These men were landed with equipment and livestock on the rocky beaches of southern Cuba. The 10th Cavalry pushed overland to where Spanish troops were dug in on El Caney hill overlooking the road leading to the city of Santiago.

A group of U. S. Cavalrymen, the "Rough Riders," had been besieged there for sixteen hours. Their leader placed his men on the right and left sides of the hill, and ordered some of the troops of the 10th Cavalry to charge up the hill from the front. They charged at the

enemy head on, meeting heavy fire. This allowed the
Rough Riders to storm up the hill on the right and the
left, with few losses.

The Rough Riders became famous and one of their
officers, Theodore Roosevelt, later was elected President. The performance of the Negro troops was praised
by all who were there.

The 10th Cavalry was not the only Negro troop
"fighting for freedom" in Cuba. On the troop ship,
Concha, heading for Cuba were 1300 men from the 14th
Infantry (white) and the 25th Infantry (Negro). The
men were segregated on the ship. The Negroes were on
the bottom deck. They slept in bunks stacked in fours,
one bunk on top of another. On the lower deck, it was
dark at noon and there were no cooling sea breezes.
These troops arrived in Cuba in time to mop up Spanish
troops beating a hasty retreat from the hill which the
Rough Riders and the 10th Cavalry had taken.

The Negro troops of the 9th Cavalry, the famous
"Black Buffaloes" of frontier days, the 10th Cavalry,
and the 24th Infantry joined the Rough Riders in taking
San Juan Hill.

Teddy Roosevelt had been a hero to many Negroes
during and after the Spanish-American War. He said,
"I don't think any Rough Rider will ever forget the tie
that binds us to the 9th and 10th Cavalry." He quoted
one of his officers, who praised the Negro cavalrymen,
saying they were "all right. They can drink out of our
canteens any day!"

*Members of the Negro 10th Cavalry charged up San Juan Hill, meet-
ing the enemy head on under heavy fire.*

However, Teddy Roosevelt did "forget the tie." Later he said Negro soldiers were "peculiarly dependent on their white officers . . . None of the white regulars or Rough Riders showed the slightest sign of weakening; but under the strain the colored infantrymen began to get a little uneasy and to drift to the rear."

To add injury *to* insult, in 1906, President Theodore Roosevelt dishonorably discharged three companies of the gallant 25th Infantry—without a hearing. These were the heroes of El Caney, Cuba. A shooting and riot had occurred in Brownsville, Texas, near their base. The events were never clear, but the men of the 25th were blamed. One fact was known: Negroes from the base who had passes in town were treated badly, made fun of, and heckled by townspeople.

Negroes could hope for little if a man who was President looked upon them with so little respect. Negro papers called him a "turncoat" and a "treacherous friend . . . who stabs you in the back."

Negroes had gone off to war thinking they would "prove" themselves by fighting for the freedom of Cuba. What of their own freedom? One Negro soldier, who later died in battle, cherished a vain hope. He had written to his wife, "Surely the same strong spirit and quickened conscience which took up the cause of Cuba will secure justice to the American Negro." But, if the leading men of the nation were touched by racist ideas, this could not be.

The U.S. came out of the Spanish-American War with Puerto Rico, the Pacific Islands of Guam, Wake, and the Philippines.

Peace Negotiation following the Spanish-American

War took place in Paris during December, 1898. The United States demanded that Spain leave the Western Hemisphere completely. Under this agreement the U.S. set Cuba free—with strong strings attached. Cuba was forced to accept an addition to her Constitution, the Platt Amendment, which gave the U.S. the "right to intervene" in Cuba's affairs and have a naval base there.

But what to do about the Philippines? Should the U.S. set them free, too?

President McKinley was uncertain about assuming the "white man's burden" in the Philippines. He explained how he had come to a decision:

"I walked the floor of the White House night after night, and I am not ashamed to tell you, gentlemen, that I went down on my knees and prayed Almighty God for light and guidance more than one night. And one night late it came to me this way . . . There was nothing left for us to do but to take them all, and to educate the Filipinos, and uplift and civilize and Christianize them . . ."

Apparently President McKinley was not aware that the Spanish, long before, had converted all Filipinos (but the Moslem Moros of the southernmost island) to Roman Catholicism!

The President felt he had no choice. He could not return the islands to Spain. "That would be cowardly and dishonorable," he said. He couldn't let Germany or some other power take them over. "That would be bad business," he said. And *certainly* he couldn't turn the islands over to the Filipinos themselves. "They were unfit for self-government," he said.

How were these new possessions to be governed? Over the years, as the U.S. expanded, the lands added were sparsely populated, usually by roving bands of Indians. The government intended that these territories would eventually join the Union as equals. Citizens of the territories were given all the rights guaranteed U.S. citizens by the Constitution, and the territories were prepared for statehood.

Americans asked themselves: What of Puerto Rico and the Philippines? Were the black and brown peoples living there entitled to the full rights of citizenship? They were of a completely different background from the mainlanders and separated from them by miles of ocean. The question was often put this way. "Does the Constitution follow the flag?"

The Supreme Court finally had to answer these questions. They did so in a series of decisions, starting in 1901. The Court decided that there were two kinds of possessions—incorporated and unincorporated. The incorporated, such as Hawaii and Alaska, were eventually to become states and their residents were entitled to Constitutional rights. The unincorporated—Puerto Rico, the Philippines, Samoa, and later the Virgin Islands— were not to become states and were not entitled to all rights. In other words, the people in the incorporated possessions would have more nearly first-class citizenship. Those of the unincorporated possessions were doomed to certain second-class citizenship.

The meaning of these decisions was clear in relation to America's colonial people at home, her nine million Negroes.

In entering the adventure of imperialism, the entire

nation seemed to be taking on the views and attitudes of the South. Now the North, too, was involved in dealings with colored peoples. White Northerners became more sympathetic and understanding of the South's "problems." In fact, the nation looked to the South for guidance on how to deal with these "new-caught, sullen peoples" on the far side of the earth.

And so these imperial adventures put the seal of approval on racism at home. The South had indeed won the Civil War!

A national magazine, *The Nation,* commented on the Supreme Court decision of 1898, one approving Mississippi's plan to deprive Negroes of their votes. *The Nation* said it was "an interesting coincidence that this important decision is rendered . . . when we are considering . . . taking in a varied assortment of inferior races in different parts of the world."

The article hastened to add that these people "of course could not be allowed to vote."

The *Atlantic Monthly,* another liberal magazine, said, "If the stronger cleverer race is free to impose its will . . . on the other side of the globe, why not in South Carolina and Mississippi?"

A delegate to the Alabama convention on Negro voting rights said, "This is not a sectional issue, the race problem is no longer confined to the States of the South." He said it was the same problem from Cuba to Alabama to Hawaii and the Philippines. Now, he said with a touch of triumph, "we have the sympathy instead of the hostility of the North."

Chapter 6

THE SLOW RISE OF JIM CROW

———◆———

"Come listen all you galls and boys,
I's jist from Tuckyhoe
I'm going to sing a little song,
My name's Jim Crow.
Weel about and turn about and do jis so,
Eb'ry time I weel about I jump Jim Crow."

These are the words of "Jim Crow" as they first appeared in sheet music around 1828, written by Thomas Dartmouth Rice. "Jim Crow" came to be more than the name of a song. The name, "Jim Crow," refers to the laws, rules, and customs that came about after Reconstruction ended. These laws governed social relations between Negroes and whites. They decreed that Negroes must go to separate schools, travel on separate trains, eat in separate restaurants, live in separate neighborhoods.

Segregation had been impossible when there was slavery. Whites and Negroes—especially slaves—had to have close contact with one another, if only to give and receive orders.

However, during slavery, a clue to the later rise of Jim Crow was the way free Negroes were treated North and South. In 1843, the state of Massachusetts had three railroads with separate—or Jim Crow—cars for Negroes.

Another clue was the Black Codes that appeared in many southern states right after the Civil War. Reconstruction struck down the Black Codes, but after the Compromise of 1877 ended Reconstruction, new laws were passed to take their place.

However, Jim Crow laws did not crop up immediately after Reconstruction. The first Jim Crow laws did not appear until 1881. And it was 20 years after Reconstruction, or 1896, before Virginia, North Carolina, and South Carolina, passed Jim Crow laws.

In Mississippi, during the early years of Reconstruction, whites and Negroes were served at the same bars. They ate in the same rooms of public eating-places, though often at separate tables. Public parks and buildings were open to both races. Negroes were sometimes kept from using the first-class railroad cars, even if they paid the price of a first-class ticket. But the second-class car was open to all regardless of race.

It took some time for Jim Crow to settle in. All the whites of the South were not of one mind on how to treat the freedmen.

The Army had already become segregated during the Civil War and had remained so. Schools and churches became segregated during Reconstruction. But as long as the Negro had the vote, white politicians still needed him. They couldn't ignore him. They had to take the Negro into account—if only to steal his vote.

So Negro voters were wooed (or threatened) first by one side, then the other. Governor Ben Tillman of

South Carolina, who later became a violent racist, in 1891 still had some respect for law and justice, because Negroes were still voters. He tried to prevent mobs from lynching Negroes in his state.

But after the Compromise of 1877, Federal troops were removed from the South, making it easier for white Southerners to take away the freedmen's vote. By 1900, Ben Tillman was a U. S. Senator, and his state had practically stripped the Negro of the vote. Tillman boldly ranted in Congress: "We have done our level best. We have scratched our heads to find out how we could eliminate the last one of them (Negro voters). We stuffed ballot boxes. We shot them. We *ARE NOT ASHAMED OF IT.*" His voice rose to a shout.

Some lone white voices still spoke out against the rising tide of Jim Crow in the 1880's.

• In New Orleans, one voice was that of the writer George Washington Cable. He had fought for the Confederacy in the Civil War. Cable wrote many articles about "the Negro problem." A book, *The Silent South,* came out in 1885. He said there could be neither free nor honest government in the South without equal rights and equal protection for all citizens—black and white. He spoke out against Jim Crow in jobs, courtrooms, voting booths, churches, schools, businesses.

He wrote, "The greatest social problem before the American people today is, as it has been for a hundred years, the presence among us of the Negro."

His statement is similar to one made a few years later by W. E. B. Du Bois, the Negro leader: "The problem of the twentieth century is the problem of the color line—the relation of the darker to the lighter races of men in Asia and Africa, in America and the islands of the sea."

• In Richmond, Lewis H. Blair published a book called *The Prosperity of the South Dependent on the Elevation of the Negro*. His book was one of the strongest pleas for civil rights ever written. Yet the author was a Southern white businessman from an old and important Richmond family. He, too, had served in the Confederate Army.

He put his ideas plainly: "The Negro must be allowed free access to all hotels and other [public] places; he must be . . . [admitted] to all theaters and other places of public amusement; he must be . . . [admitted] to all churches, and in all public and official receptions . . . In all these things . . . he must . . . be treated precisely like the whites, not better, but no worse."

In 1898 Blair was still calling for equality. But sometime after that his ideas changed. Blair, too, was swept away by the tide of Jim Crow. His change of mind matched what was happening in the U.S. No one really knows what brought on his about-face. He left no record of how the change came about. It remains a tragic mystery.

• In Georgia, Tom Watson was a leader of poor white farmers. He, too, was later swept away by Jim Crow, but in the 1880's and '90's he worked for understanding and cooperation between the Negro and white farmers of the South.

His group was called the Populists. Times were bad on farms in the 1880's and '90's. The country as a whole was going through a depression. Thousands of businesses failed. Factories closed. Several million workers were unemployed. The prices of farm goods dropped sharply.

Farmers could not afford to pay the cost of shipping crops to market. They lost money because the prices they were paid did not cover the cost of freight. Since the farmers were not making a profit, they couldn't afford to buy goods produced by factories. That made even more businesses and factories fail.

The poor white farmers and workers were discontented with the policies of the Democratic party. They felt that both major parties had failed to deal with the problems of the poor. They began to organize what was later called the Populist (people's) party.

The poor farmer, Negro or white, shared many of the same problems. They had common enemies—the landlord and the storekeeper. Populists considered it common sense for Negroes and whites to work together. A Populist group in the South, the Southern Farmer's Alliance, had three million members. It asked the Colored Alliance, which had one and a quarter million members and branches in 20 states, to cooperate with them.

Tom Watson, the leader of the Populists, promised Negro voters, "If you stand up for your rights and your manhood, if you stand shoulder to shoulder with us in this fight [we will] wipe out the color line."

This was a brave promise for those times. He tried to insert a statement against lynching into the Populist party platform. He did this at a time when his home state, Georgia, had lynched more Negroes than any other state. Populist leaders were working against great odds. The very people they were trying to get to work with the Negroes were the poorest whites. They were the ones who most feared the competition of Negro farmers and workers. Poor whites and Negroes were rivals. They both wanted jobs in mines and mills.

Even so, the Populists made surprising headway with their arguments that blacks and whites were stronger together. A Negro delegate frankly told a meeting of Populists in Texas: "The Negro vote will be the balancing vote in Texas. If you are going to win, you will have to take the Negro vote with you . . . You must appoint us by conventions and make us feel that we are men."

For a few years, in the 1890's, Negroes and whites worked side by side in the Populist party. Negro and white candidates campaigned from the same platform. They spoke to mixed audiences. Their names appeared on the same party ticket. Populist sheriffs saw to it that Negroes were called up for jury duty.

From 1894–98, North Carolina's government was in the hands of a combination of white Populists and Negro Republicans. During this time they improved education, gave more people the right to vote, made the tax system fairer. Negroes held a number of public offices.

The Populists had split off the poor white farmers from the Democratic party. The Populist party represented the interests of the farmers, while the Democrats appealed to the South's bankers, merchants, manufacturers, and railroad owners. Both Democrats and Popu-

Tom Watson, leader of the Populists, promised Negro voters, "If you stand shoulder to shoulder with us in this fight [we will] wipe out the color line."

lists wanted the support of the Negro voter. He became for a while the balance of power in elections. Both sides needed his vote in order to win. The parties did many things—some dishonest—to make sure they received the Negro vote.

Practices ranged from threats, to cheating, to buying votes, to making voting complicated and confusing. Ballot boxes were stuffed with extra ballots marked for the "right" candidate. False bottoms were used on some ballot boxes, so that ballots could be examined and votes for the "wrong" candidate dropped out. Officials let people vote more than once if they voted "right."

The following exchange in the Arkansas House of Representatives in 1889 was reported in a Little Rock, Arkansas, paper:

—"I ask if there is a member on this floor who will pretend to deny that nine ballot-boxes were stolen from the clerk's office in . . . [Pulaski] County," demanded the Speaker of the House.

—"Only six were stolen," the Representative from Pulaski stoutly defended his county.

—"Very well, I stand corrected," the Speaker replied. "Only six ballot boxes and poll books were stolen from . . . the county in which stands the capitol of the beloved Arkansas."

The Southern states said taking away the Negro's vote would put an end to this cheating. Concern about unfair elections and cheating masked a deeper fear. Poor white farmers and laborers were joining the Populist party and were pressing for more power in Southern politics and for a better chance to earn a decent living.

Wealthy whites were alarmed at these demands. Landless Negroes and poor whites were beginning to cooperate in the Populist movement. If the Populist movement should really work, a true Negro-white alliance might form. Political power would then be out of the control of the wealthy class of Southern white men forever.

Chapter 7

SEPARATE AND NOT EQUAL

———◆———

Southerners feared that Negro and poor whites would work together, but this did not happen. Many Negroes continued to look toward middle and upper class whites out of habit. They regarded them as protectors. They had long dealt with and felt closer to the class of people that had been their masters before the Civil War. They also depended on planters, merchants, and mill and mine owners for jobs. They looked with suspicion upon the poor whites who had been overseers on the plantations. Very often they had used brutal ways to keep order among the slaves. In the years after the Civil War, these were the people who had joined bands of night riders and terrorized the Negro communities, and they now competed with the freedmen for jobs and land.

The Populists were disillusioned. They expected the wholehearted support and trust of the Negro and they did not get it. They turned against the Negroes and began to say that the alliance would never work.

The Populists and upper class whites stopped fighting one another, closed ranks and reunited. They agreed to take away the Negro's vote so that the freedmen could no longer swing an election one way or another. Whites would then be able to decide the issues about jobs and land without giving Negroes a voice in their own interests.

Mississippi was the first state to take away the Negro vote. This practice was known as *disfranchisement*. (Franchise is another word for vote.) In 1890, Mississippi held a convention to draw up a new constitution for the state. The main purpose was to write in ways of disfranchising Negroes.

The disfranchisers faced two big obstacles:

• how to get around the Fifteenth Amendment that forbade discrimination on the basis of "race, color, or previous condition of servitude."

• how to prevent poor and uneducated Negroes from voting, while allowing poor and uneducated whites to vote.

The laws passed to keep Negroes from voting dealt mainly with property and education:

Property. To vote a man generally had to own property worth from $300 to $500. Few freedmen had been able to acquire land and other property.

Education. Voters had to take literacy tests to prove they could read and write. Many Negroes had long been kept from getting an education.

Poll Taxes. As much as eighteen months to two years before an election, a would-be voter had to register to vote. He had to pay a tax of a few dollars, for which he received a receipt. He would have to save this receipt to show on election day. A poll tax might be only a few dollars a year. But in order to vote in a certain year, a man would have to pay up for past years. This could

FORD COUNTY
DEMOCRATIC
PRIMARY

November 3, 188

*One effective way of stopping the stealing of bal-
lots . . . is to stop the people from casting them.*

add up to a sizeable sum. It was usually beyond the means of a poor sharecropper who earned less than a hundred dollars a year and was probably in debt to the storekeeper.

Residence Requirements. Another law ruled that a man had to live in one place for several years before he could vote there. Many poor Negroes had to move often in search of work. Sometimes they didn't stay in one town long enough to meet the long residence requirements.

Many of these laws also stopped white voters. Loopholes were set up that would disqualify Negroes but would allow poor and illiterate white men to vote:

• "Understanding Clauses." People who could not read and write could not pass a literacy test—but perhaps they could "understand." To test their understanding, the voting registrar would read aloud a section of the state constitution. Then he would ask the would-be voter to explain what had been read to him. If he could "understand," he was allowed to register to vote. If a Negro so much as misspelled a word or left out a comma, he could fail the literacy test. But officials would look the other way if a white man made the same mistake, and would apply the understanding clause to allow him to vote.

• "Grandfather Clauses." If a man or his father or grandfather had voted before January 1, 1867, then the man himself was entitled to vote. This protected voting privileges for white persons who would have lost their vote if judged on the same basis as Negroes. Negroes could not take advantage of this loophole since they had been barred from voting before 1867.

In 1898, the Mississippi Plan gained the approval of the Supreme Court. Other Southern states quickly lined up behind Mississippi to deprive the Negro of his vote. Each state, by 1910, had worked out some variation of this plan.

The Mississippi Plan and the others like it were effective in depriving Negroes of the vote. In Louisiana, for instance, 130,334 Negroes were registered to vote in 1896. Then poll taxes, literacy tests, and property qualifications went into effect, and Negro voters numbered 5320 in 1900. By 1904, the number had dropped to 1342. With the loss of voting power, the Negro practically disappeared from the political scene. George H. White of North Carolina, whose term ended in 1901, was the last Negro to serve in Congress until 1928.

After disfranchisement, the Negroes had no way to defend themselves when white mobs rioted against them. Without the vote, Negroes could not elect officials who would uphold their rights and prevent the spread of Jim Crow.

The whites had taken away the Negro's vote, yet the Negro was not left alone. Instead, some of the worst riots broke out *after* the Negro was no longer a "threat" as a voter.

In 1898, a candidate who believed in white supremacy won in North Carolina. Shortly after, a mob of four hundred white men, led by a former Congressman, swooped down on the Negro district of Wilmington. They set fire to buildings, wounded and killed many Negroes and drove hundreds out of town.

In 1900, white mobs roamed the city of New Orleans for three days looting, shooting, and burning.

In 1906, a white supremist won an election in Georgia. The election was followed by a four-day riot. White mobs roamed the streets, stealing and lynching.

Rioting in the North was almost as vicious and violent as in the South. In 1900, in a single month, riots broke out in New York City and Akron, Ohio. In 1908, mobs rioted for two days in Springfield, Illinois, Lincoln's home town. They attacked Negroes, crying, "Lincoln freed you; we'll show you where you belong!"

Jim Crow went hand in hand with disfranchisement. And because the idea that Negroes were inferior was so widely held at the time, the Federal government did nothing to stop the growth of Jim Crow laws.

Tennessee led off, with a Jim Crow law for railroads in 1881. Florida followed in 1887. One law led to a hundred laws. Signs appeared:

| WHITE |

| COLORED |

| NEGROES AND FREIGHT |

White nurses were forbidden by law to treat Negroes. White teachers couldn't teach Negro pupils. South Carolina forbade black and white cotton mill workers from looking out of the same windows. Florida had "Negro" and "white" textbooks—which were stored separately in warehouses! Oklahoma, in 1915, passed a law calling for "separate but equal" phone booths.

Three states had Jim Crow waiting rooms before

Negroes and whites were separated in public transportation, at sports events, in theaters, hospitals, prisons, orphanages, and asylums.

1899. In the next few years, other states fell into the Jim Crow lineup. Before 1900, only Georgia had Jim Crow seats on streetcars. North Carolina and Virginia passed streetcar laws in 1901, Louisiana in 1902, Arkansas, South Carolina, and Tennessee in 1903, Mississippi and Maryland in 1904, and Florida in 1905.

Each year brought some new Jim Crow law or some new twist to old ones. Mobile, Alabama, said Negroes had to be off the streets by 10 P.M. In Birmingham, Negroes and whites couldn't play checkers together. Negroes and whites were separated in public transportation, at sports events, in theaters, hospitals, prisons, orphanages, and asylums. Even the blind were separated by color at state institutions. As Negroes moved from farms to cities, Jim Crow neighborhoods grew up in both Northern and Southern cities.

Lynchings had been common in the South in the 1830's, '40's, and '50's. Most of the people lynched then were whites. Negro lynchings began at the time of Reconstruction, first, to punish and frighten the freedmen as a group, and then to keep the Negroes from voting and to enforce Jim Crow. In the 1890's called the "Terrible Nineties," a Negro was lynched somewhere in the South every two days. There were 230 lynchings in 1892 alone. From 1882 to 1959, there were 4735 lynchings in the U.S.

In 1896, the U. S. Supreme Court handed down a famous decision affecting Jim Crow laws. This decision, *Plessy v. Ferguson*, said that Jim Crow laws were not unconstitutional.

The case concerned a law passed by Louisiana in

1890, forbidding Negroes and whites to ride together in the same railroad car. Homer Plessy, a Negro, decided to challenge the law. He considered it his right, as a man, to ride in any car he chose. He entered a car reserved FOR WHITES ONLY. When the conductor asked him to move, he refused and was arrested.

Plessy's lawyers argued that to forbid him from riding in the all-white car marked him as inferior—as less of a man—than a white passenger. The opposing lawyers argued that separate cars for Negroes was not a mark of inferiority—as long as the cars were "equal."

The Supreme Court decided eight to one that the Louisiana law did not go against the Constitution.

The Court put the Fourteenth Amendment, originally intended to protect the rights of freedmen, to a completely different use.

The Fourteenth Amendment, passed in 1868, is the basis of most civil rights cases to this day. It reads in part:

"No state shall make or enforce any law which shall abridge the privileges or immunities of citizens of the United States; nor shall any state deprive any person of life, liberty, or property without due process of law; nor deny to any person within its jurisdiction the equal protection of the law."

The Court agreed that the Fourteenth Amendment was intended to make the two races "equal" before the law.

The Court said that laws requiring segregation did not mean that either race was inferior. However, it went on to say that "If one race be inferior to the other socially, the Constitution of the United States cannot put them on the same plane. The distinction between the two races . . . founded on the color of the two races, must always exist so long as white men are distinct from the other color."

Justice John Marshall Harlan cast the lone "no" vote. A former slaveholder from the border state of Kentucky, Harlan had fought on the Union side in the Civil War. He wrote a stinging dissent to the majority decision.

He said that Jim Crow laws encouraged state and local governments to further whittle away the rights of Negroes. He scolded his fellow Justices for their interpretation of the Constitution:

"Our Constitution is color-blind, and neither knows nor tolerates classes among citizens . . . The law regards man as man, and takes no account of his surroundings or of his color . . .

"We boast of the freedom enjoyed by our people above all other peoples. But it is difficult to reconcile that boast with a state of the law which . . . puts the brand of servitude and degradation upon a large class of our fellow-citizens."

And so the rule of "separate but equal" was installed as the law of the land.

What did "equal" mean? Did it mean that the railroad cars had to look the same, have the same number of seats, have the same kind of upholstery?

What did it mean to have "separate but equal" schools? Did it mean that the books would be identical? That the course of study would be the same? Did it mean that the same amount of money would be spent in each school? (In former slave states, at that time, four to five times more money was spent on educating the average white child.)

As Justice Harlan predicted, the *Plessy v. Ferguson* decision gave the go-ahead signal to Southern states to install Jim Crow by law.

Chapter 8

A BARGAIN AT ATLANTA

———◆———

THE TIME: September 18, 1895
THE PLACE: Cotton States and International Exposition Building, Atlanta, Georgia
THE SCENE: ". . . A remarkable figure [rose to speak]; tall, bony, straight as a Sioux chief, high forehead, straight nose, heavy jaws, and strong determined mouth . . . piercing eyes, and a commanding manner . . . His voice rang out clear and true, and he paused impressively as he made each point. Within ten minutes, the multitude was in an uproar of enthusiasm—handkerchiefs were waved, canes were flourished, hats were tossed in the air. The fairest women of Georgia stood up and cheered . . ."

That was the report filed by James Creelman, the correspondent for the New York *World*. He was describing Professor Booker T. Washington, principal of Tuskegee Institute in Alabama.

Professor Washington told the audience that the Negro, starting with so little, would have to work up gradually before he would have power or position in the South.

"Ignorant and inexperienced, it is not strange that in the first years of our new life we began at the top instead at the bottom; that a seat in Congress or the

State Legislature was more sought than real estate or industrial skill; that the political convention or stump speaking had more attractions than starting a dairy farm or truck garden."

He advised his fellow Negroes in the South to make friends with the "Southern white man, who is his next door neighbor." He urged Negroes to work with their hands—as farmers, mechanics, and domestic servants. He warned:

"No race can prosper till it learns that there is as much dignity in tilling a field as in writing a poem. It is at the bottom of life we must begin and not at the top. . ."

Then came the high point—Washington held his hand above his head, fingers stretched wide apart. He promised:

"In all things that are purely social we can be as separate as the fingers, yet one as the hand in all things essential to mutual progress."

The audience cheered frantically. Even now, that sentence is the most quoted one of Washington's Atlanta speech. With it he seemed to surrender the Negroes' hopes of becoming first-class citizens, and he opened wide the door to Jim Crow.

After the cheering stopped, Professor Washington went on—speaking for millions of black people who had never been asked what they thought. In the name of all Negroes, he gave up the ideal of social equality.

Though he felt it was important that "all privileges of the law be ours." he thought it was far more important to "be prepared for the exercise of those privileges. The opportunity to earn a dollar in a factory just now

is worth infinitely more than the opportunity to spend a dollar in an opera house."

The New York reporter, Mr. Creelman, wrote that at the end of the speech, "most of the Negroes in the audience were crying, perhaps without knowing why."

Booker T. Washington's invitation to speak was made by a group of Southern businessmen. They had organized the Cotton States Exposition to help heal the rift between North and South and to attract more business and trade. They invited exhibitors from all 46 states and from foreign countries.

Before asking Booker T. Washington to speak, the businessmen had debated a long time. After all, they said, he was a Negro. What would he say? Would he embarrass the white South before the North and the world? They thought not. They trusted Professor Washington to do what they thought was right.

He had come to Alabama in 1881 to head Tuskegee Institute. Starting with nothing but the $2000 a year granted by the Alabama State Legislature and two rickety buildings with leaks in the roofs, he built the school into a well-known institution.

Washington's aim was to find a way to improve the lot of his people. He believed that the best way to do this was to teach them useful skills and trades. He thought academic subjects—Latin, literature, French, history, art, mathematics—would not help men on the lowest rung of the ladder. First they should learn to work with their hands. If they did this, he was con-

"In all things that are purely social we can be as separate as the fingers, yet one as the hand in all things essential to mutual progress."

vinced, the children of slaves would "work their way to the top."

Booker T. Washington firmly believed in a "gospel of Work and Money," as W. E. B. Du Bois put it. Tuskegee was the place where he carried out these beliefs. The class of 1886 had this motto: "There is Room at the Top."

The Tuskegee plan fit right in with ideas popular with much of the nation—especially with the driving and energetic businessmen and industrialists of the North. It was thrift, hard work, and the "almighty dollar" that made the world go round. Booker T. Washington once said, "There is little race prejudice in the American dollar."

At Tuskegee young people were taught to work with their hands. They learned to take pride in their handwork. The young Negroes were encouraged to be orderly, obedient, clean, and cooperative. These traits and skills were useful for the Negro in many ways. At the same time, they certainly fit in with the Southern notion of the Negro as a servant and laborer. They fit in with the Northern industrialist's dream of an unlimited supply of humble, loyal workers who did not belong to unions.

Mr. Washington urged Negroes to "suffer in silence" about race prejudice and injustice. He said he had learned long ago that "it does not pay to disturb" prejudices, and that the South should be left alone to solve its "Negro problem."

He told Southerners what they very much wanted to hear, and he reassured the North that the race troubles of the South would be settled. That was why he was invited to speak at Atlanta.

His ideas had worked well for the white businessmen and factory builders who were amassing fortunes. But would they work for the millions of Negroes just 30 years out of slavery? Washington hoped that they would. He was counting on this hope when he made his bargain at Atlanta.

Washington considered it his life work to find a "reasonable" compromise among the Negroes, the Northern whites, and the Southern whites. And it was looked upon as a huge triumph that he could—at a time when feelings ran so high—say things that the majority of the nation could even partly agree on.

The newspapers of the South enthusiastically approved the speech. He was hailed as a leader and a statesman, a truly "sensible" man.

Many Northern papers, too, thought Booker T. Washington was on the right road. A Chicago paper said:

"If every southern state had such an institution as that at Tuskegee, Alabama, presided over by such a man as Professor Washington, the race question would settle itself in ten years."

Only one Northern paper, the Detroit *Tribune*, pointed out the difference between Washington's bright hopes for the South and what was really happening there. "The latest Tennessee lynching should be exhibited at the Atlanta Exposition as a fine specimen of one of the staple products of the South."

His Atlanta speech brought Booker T. Washington

great fame. From that time on he was one of the great and powerful men of the nation. Industrialists and Presidents sought his advice. He was the first Negro to have dinner with a President at the White House. (This, however, stirred a storm in the South. A paper wrote, "God set up a barrier between the races. No President of this or any country can break it down.") Presidents Theodore Roosevelt and William Howard Taft consulted him on every appointment of a Negro to a government position. Often, they spoke with him before naming Southern white men to office.

He was looked upon as the leading Negro spokesman from 1895 until his death in 1915. What he said set the tone—for whites and Negroes—for many years to come. It had powerful effects on race relations in the United States. Some other Negro leaders followed his example. Later, many laws of Congress, acts of Presidents, and Supreme Court decisions were to reflect the point of view of his Atlanta speech.

The speech was later referred to as the "Atlanta Compromise." It was a bargain made among Negroes, Southern whites, and Northern businessmen.

Booker T. Washington promised that Negroes would put off their hopes for equal rights in exchange for a chance to earn a better living and to get an education. Their willingness to wait for equality would presumably bring peace to the South, and Northern businessmen would feel safe to invest their money in the steel, coal, cotton, and lumber of the South. The South would prosper. And the grateful South would eventually award the Negro his rights. That was the way it was *supposed* to work.

Booker T. Washington may have thought he was making the best of a bad situation. He was convinced that the Negro would not get his equal rights in U.S.A. 1895 by asking for them.

Mr. Washington's Atlanta bargain brought many unwanted results. Instead of peace, the Negro was rewarded with a loss of his right to vote, fewer and lower paying jobs, inferior schools, increased segregation, and a rise in lynchings.

The skills Negroes were learning at Tuskegee and other schools were becoming useless in the modern industrial world. Wheelwrighting, for instance, was a skill suitable to the Old South of Booker T. Washington's boyhood—not to the New South with its steel mills.

In these new steel mills and cotton factories, built by Booker T. Washington's wealthy Northern friends, Negroes worked as janitors. Jobs became strictly classified as white men's jobs and black men's jobs. Negroes' jobs were generally the hardest, heaviest, dirtiest, and lowest-paying. Saw mills, coal mines, and building and repairing railroads came to be black men's industries in the New South.

Booker T. Washington thought that the only way Negroes could survive in a hostile society was by being meek and mild. He did not seem to understand the awful human cost of submission. He did not seem to understand the awful damage that it did to a man's pride, his belief in himself.

After his death in 1915, an article he wrote was published in *The New Republic*. He told what segregation meant to the Negro:

"Inferior accommodations in return for the taxes he

pays . . . that the sewerage in his part of the city will
be inferior; that the streets and sidewalks will be neglected; that the street lighting will be poor; that his
section of the city will not be kept in order by the police
and other authorities, and that . . . it will be difficult
for him to rear his family in decency."

These are the harsh, plain words that Booker T.
Washington never spoke publicly in his lifetime.

Some other people of his time saw things differently
—and spoke up. They feared what the future would
bring if the Negro gave up his rights. Frederick
Douglass was one of these. But he died in 1895, the
very year that Washington made this compromise.

John Hope, who had once turned down a job at
Tuskegee and later became president of Atlanta University, was in the audience at Atlanta when Booker T.
Washington gave his speech. John Hope thought a long
time about what was said. Then on February 22 of the
next year, he replied, saying:

"If we are not striving for equality, in heaven's name
for what are we living? I regard it as cowardly and
dishonest for any of our colored men to tell white people
or colored people that we are not struggling for equality . . . Let us not fool ourselves nor be fooled by
others. If we cannot do what other freemen do, then
we are not free. Yes, my friends, I want equality. Nothing less . . .

"Now catch your breath, for I am going . . . to say
we demand social equality . . .

"Rise Brothers! . . . Never say 'Let well enough
alone' . . . Be discontented. Be dissatisfied . . . Let
your discontent break mountain-high against the wall

of prejudice, and swamp it . . . Then we shall not have to plead for justice nor on bended knee crave mercy; for we shall be men . . ."

Another opponent of Booker T. Washington's was William Edward Burghardt Du Bois. Born in Massachusetts in 1868, he was the great-great-grandson of a slave who had won his own freedom by fighting in the American Revolutionary War. Du Bois was educated at Fisk, Harvard, and the University of Berlin (Germany). He was the first Negro to receive a Ph.D. (Doctor of Philosophy) from Harvard.

In 1903 he published a book of essays called *The Souls of Black Folk*. Even the title was shocking to some people at that time. One of the essays attacked Washington's policy of depending solely on the "good will" of white folks. Dr. Du Bois urged Negro leaders to demand every right that was theirs.

He pointed out that Mr. Washington asked black people to give up three things:

"First, political power,
"Second, insistence on civil rights,
"Third, higher education of Negro youth . . ."

Dr. Du Bois turned around and said that Negroes must ask the nation for these very things:

"1. The right to vote
"2. Civic equality
"3. The education of youth according to ability."

He closed his essay saying:

"By every civilized and peaceful method we must strive for the rights which the world accords to men, clinging unwaveringly to those great words (from the Declaration of Independence) . . . : 'We hold these truths to be self evident: That all men are created equal, that they are endowed by their Creator with certain unalienable rights; that among these are life, liberty, and the pursuit of happiness.'"

In a short time, W. E. B. Du Bois and others would join to act on these proud words. A new kind of Negro leadership was "blowin' in the wind." But there would also be more "sorrow songs."

Chapter 9

ON THE MOVE

Life for the Negro in the United States had reached its lowest point since Reconstruction. In fact, this time has been called the "nadir."

No one can say exactly when the slow climb up from the nadir began. But certain clues pointed toward a change. A new mood was in the air.

Riots, lynchings, and countless daily humiliations continued long into the twentieth century. But a new spirit was rising among Negroes. A "New Negro" was being born. In 1895, even while his Atlanta speech was helping to strengthen the Negroes' bondage, Booker T. Washington had started to talk and write about a "New Negro." He may not have known how this "New Negro" would turn out, but the phrase caught on.

Many Americans—black and white—still believed in the ringing words of their Declaration of Independence: "All men are created equal . . ." They still paid lip service to the ideals of equality and the right to "life, liberty, and the pursuit of happiness." These ideals were not always acted upon, but they were talked about as being the "right thing" to do. They were still considered "the American way."

The ideals had not died. Many people took them seriously and began to question the gap between what actually was and what was only talked about. The seeds of change lay with these people who questioned and then began to act. They helped start the long climb up from the nadir.

Much of the energy for the climb came from the Negro himself. Despite all the cards being stacked against him—poor schools, no land, Jim Crow, disfranchisement—the Negro had made gains.

In 1865, only one out of every ten Negroes could read and write. By the early 1900's, about 6 out of every 10 Negroes could. Negroes were making gains in art, science, literature, music. By 1900 there were 21,267 teachers, 15,528 preachers, 1734 doctors, 212 dentists, 310 journalists, 728 lawyers, 2000 actors and show people, 236 artists, 247 photographers.

Many Negro artists went to Europe, where they were discovered and gained fame. One such artist was Henry Ossawa Tanner, whose painting, "The Resurrection of Lazarus," was the sensation of the Paris Exhibition of 1897.

Charles Waddell Chesnutt wrote novels exposing the evil and destructive side of plantation life. His novels honestly treated relationships between Negroes and whites and between Negroes of different classes.

Paul Laurence Dunbar wrote novels and poetry. Many of his poems spoke deeply and movingly of the inner agony of the Negro in America. One poem opens with these lines:

> "We wear the mask that grins and lies,
>   It hides our cheeks and shades our eyes,—
>   . . . . .
> With torn and bleeding hearts we smile."

As far back as 1882, a two-volume *History of the Negro Race in America* was written by George Washington Williams. Filled with facts and figures about Negro life in America, it became a useful reference book for later historians.

Another source of energy for the climb from the nadir came from Negro newspapers and magazines. Most white papers ignored or belittled the Negro; the Negro community desperately needed papers that would speak strongly for Negroes and to them.

In 1890 there were 150 weekly Negro newspapers. Some didn't last long. Others reported only society news. But some became outspoken voices of the Negro people.

One of the most militant newsmen was T. Thomas Fortune, a fiery-tempered man who edited first the *Globe,* then the *Freeman,* and finally the New York *Age.*

Another outspoken editor was William Monroe Trotter. Like Du Bois, he was from New England. The two had roomed together while at Harvard University. Trotter founded the Boston *Guardian* in 1901. His editorial stand was "freedom now." He violently objected to Booker T. Washington's point of view. In a *Guardian* editorial, Trotter called him a "Jim Crowist" and a "prophet of slavery and traitor to [his] race."

Negroes had started joining together in groups to protest. In 1890, Negroes from 21 states and the District of Columbia met in Chicago to form the Afro-American League. They called for an equal share of schools funds, fair trials for Negroes, resistance "by all legal and reasonable means" to mobs and lynchings, and the right to vote for all those qualified.

Negro churches often became community centers. The segregated churches were a haven for Negroes. Ministers did not depend on the white community and could afford to be independent. They were free to serve only their Negro parishioners. And they did serve them in many ways, as leaders, teachers, advisers. In many small country towns no one else could fill the minister's shoes. The churches became a center of hope and of refuge, and eventually a place of protest.

Negro businesses played some part in the upswing. Washington had high hopes that business success was the surest road to the top for his people. He organized the National Negro Business League in 1900. But most Negroes lacked money to invest in businesses. They found it hard to compete with large, well-established white businesses. Small businesses of any kind—whether owned by blacks or whites—had trouble succeeding. Bigger companies were more likely to survive.

Those Negro businesses geared mostly to serve Negro trade succeeded. White undertakers, insurance companies, beauty parlors, and barber shops often refused to serve Negroes. Negroes who went into these businesses did prosper.

All these things together gave Negroes a boost. A more militant mood was growing among Negroes. The daily insults, the horrors of riots and lynchings had to be stopped. *Something had to be done.*

No matter what they tried to do, the mass of Negroes had little hope of changing the situation and bettering themselves. The daily insults were bad enough. But long-term goals and hopes were cut off, too. Negroes were denied good schools, decent homes, and most skilled jobs. Negroes strongly felt the need to overcome their frustration and hopelessness. *Something had to be done.*

It was heartbreaking when the President himself (William Howard Taft) did not believe that Negroes and whites could live in peace and brotherhood in the United States. He said in a speech to Negro students at a college in Charlotte, North Carolina, that the only way to solve the "race problem" was to deport Negroes. He concluded his talk with this pronouncement: "Your race is adapted to be a race of farmers, first, last, and for all times." *Something had to be done.*

Negroes who had followed Washington's prescription of thrift, hard work, and compromise found that the roadblocks were still up for them, too. After the Atlanta riots of 1906, a Negro doctor, W. F. Penn, a graduate of Yale, spoke before a meeting of whites. He told them that the mob had broken into his home, threatened his family, and nearly killed him. Dr. Penn despaired:

"We have been disarmed: how shall we protect our lives and property? If living a sober, industrious, upright life, accumulating property and educating his children . . . is not the standard by which a colored man can live and be protected in the South, what is to become of him? If the kind of life I have lived isn't the kind you want, shall I leave and go North?"

Atlanta's "good people" were properly horrified. Ashamed of the actions of their white neighbors, they set up a relief fund for the victims of the riots. This was a start, but it certainly was not an answer to Dr. Penn's deeply serious question. *Something had to be done.*

A Negro woman wrote a letter which was printed in a national magazine, *The Independent,* in 1902. She told of how little whites knew about Negroes—and the results of this ignorance. Part of her letter reads:

"The Southerners say we Negroes are a happy, laughing set of people, with no thought of tomorrow. How mistaken they are! The educated, thinking Negro is just the opposite. There is a feeling of unrest, insecurity, almost panic among the best class of Negroes in the South. In our homes, in our churches, wherever two or three are gathered together, there is a discussion of what is best to do. Must we remain in the South or go elsewhere? Where can we go to feel that security which other people feel? Is it best to go in great numbers or only several families? These and other things are discussed over and over . . ."

What was the Negro to do? Where was he to go? At different times during the 1800's and continuing into the 1900's, various movements were begun: Go North, Go West, Go Back to Africa. Negro leaders were strongly divided on the wisdom of moving from the South. Frederick Douglass, during the big move to Kansas in 1879, had advised against it. He said running away wouldn't solve the problem. In 1895, Booker T. Washington had advised Negroes to "cast down your bucket where you are" (in the South).

But Negroes had little hope that their life would change, especially on Southern farms. They were doomed to poverty and back-breaking work, always to be tenant farmers, sharecroppers, or farm laborers. Their very lives were not even safe.

W. E. B. Du Bois was teaching at Atlanta University

at the time of the 1906 riots. The riots convinced him the Negro should leave the South. Du Bois spoke out:

"We might as well face the facts squarely; if there is any colored man in the South who wishes to have his children educated and who wishes to be in close touch with civilization and who has any ghost of a chance of making a living in the North it is his business to get out of the South as soon as possible . . . The only effective protest that the Negroes . . . can make against lynching and disfranchisement is through leaving the devilish country where these things take place."

A move was underway. First it was from one part of the South to another—from one farm to another, from country to town, from town to city. Sometimes Negroes moved from poorer, worn-out lands in the older states along the eastern coast to richer, fresher lands in the newer states farther west.

A steady stream of Negroes moved to the cities of the North. This did not amount to huge numbers of people until around World War I. In 1900, all but 900,000 Negroes lived in the South. Even in 1913, 50 years after Emancipation, nine-tenths of U. S. Negroes still lived in the South.

Conditions for the Negro were not much better outside the South. The Negroes who fled North had a hard time finding places to live in Northern cities. They competed for homes and jobs with poor immigrants who were pouring in from Southern and Eastern Europe at the same time. For example, there arrived in Chicago between 1900 and 1910: 30,000 Italians, 120,000 Russians, 24,000 Hungarians, and 5000 Greeks.

In the 1890's there were 15,000 Negroes in Chicago.

A steady stream of Negroes moved to the cities of the North.

They were squeezed into a narrow strip between a well-off white neighborhood and one where poor Irish immigrants lived. By 1908, 45,000 Negroes lived in Chicago.

In the 1890's, 23,000 Negroes were scattered in different parts of New York City. By 1900 their numbers had doubled. And in 1903, a Negro real estate man offered to fill vacancies in the section of the city called Harlem with Negro tenants. Harlem had once been a wealthy white neighborhood.

At first the move of Negroes into Harlem was a slow, quiet trickle. Whites living there paid little attention. As the trickle became a torrent, panic grew among the whites, and they moved out.

James Weldon Johnson, the Negro poet, teacher, diplomat, and musician, was living in New York then. He said the whites "began fleeing as from a plague. The presence of one colored family on a block, no matter how well bred and orderly, was sufficient to precipitate [set off] a flight. House after house and block after block was actually deserted."

Soon Negroes, unable to find places to live in other neighborhoods, flocked into Harlem. Single family homes were divided into rooming houses and apartments. Several Negro families might be crowded into the same space in which a single white family had lived.

By 1910, almost three-quarters of a million Negroes lived in three cities—New York, Chicago, and Philadelphia. They accounted for a fifth of all Negroes in the North.

Southerners began to realize they were losing their source of cheap labor. The Atlanta *Constitution* said:

"There is no secret about what must be done if Georgia would save herself from threatened disaster. There must be no more mobs . . . We must be fair to the Negro. We have not shown that fairness in the past, nor are we showing it today, either in justice before the law . . . or [elsewhere]."

Negroes were not men, but "valuable assets"—a carry-over from slave times when they were pieces of property to be valued as such.

Between the years 1906 and 1908, a newspaperman, Ray Stannard Baker, wrote a pioneer piece of work. He was the first white journalist to explore thoroughly race relations in the North and South. He wrote his articles for the *American Magazine*. The articles became a book, *Following the Color Line*.

"It keeps coming to me that this is more a white man's problem than it is a Negro problem," Baker wrote. He believed that what whites were doing to Negroes would eventually taint all of American life.

For two years, Baker traveled, studied, and wrote articles, always "following the color line." He started in 1906, only one week after the Atlanta riots. He witnessed lynch mobs in action, interviewed white and Negro leaders, and talked to men and women in the street.

He tried to explain the growing gap between the views of Booker T. Washington and Du Bois.

Baker did much research on why Negroes were starting to move to Northern cities. He found that Negroes in small towns and on farms complained about poor schools and the lack of protection from attacks by white racists.

One Mississippi man heading for Indianapolis told

him, "They're Jim Crowin' us down here too much. There's no chance for a colored man who has any self-respect."

Baker wrote that Negroes *felt* free in Northern cities. "No people, either black or white, are really free until they feel free," he wrote. "And to many Negroes the first few weeks in a Northern city gives them the first glimpses they have ever had of what they consider to be liberty."

"But, soon they begin to learn things!" They learn about high rents; the high cost of food; the need for more fuel and heavier clothing for harsh northern winters. They learn that there are white men's jobs and black men's jobs in the North, too.

Even so, a Negro minister in Philadelphia told Baker, "Well, they're treated more like men up here . . . that's the secret of it. There's prejudice here, too, but the color line isn't drawn in their faces at every turn as it is in the South. It all gets back to a question of manhood."

Despite his sympathy, fairness, and unusual understanding of the problem, Baker was not ready for fiery militancy. He favored Washington's philosophy. Washington said, "We ought to confine ourselves largely to things that lie within our power to remedy. We can overcome prejudice in a quiet patient way . . ."

Baker said a "wise Southerner" had told him that the solution to "the Negro problem [was] Time and Patience."

But there were some Negroes who had little time and no more patience left. They were starting to act.

Chapter 10

"TO BE BOTH A NEGRO AND AN AMERICAN"

"High on a magnificent promontory, out of a mist, a hundred people gathered at early dawn. They formed a procession and moved forward with evident purpose. The light grew and shown upon their faces. They were Negroes. They were on a solemn pilgrimage. They were barefooted in sign of their reverence and profound dedication . . . Their cause was to find justice in their native land."

This description appeared in the biography of John Hope, the president of Atlanta University. He was one of a hundred Negro militants—teachers, ministers, businessmen, writers—who met at Harpers Ferry, West Virginia, in August 1906. This was the second meeting of the Niagara Movement. It took its name from the place of the first meeting.

In 1905, the group had answered a call for "aggressive action" from W. E. B. Du Bois and William Monroe Trotter. They met at Fort Erie, Ontario, on the Canadian side of Niagara Falls.

The Niagara group met in places sacred to the cause of Negro freedom. Fort Erie had been a last stop on the Underground Railroad. It was here slaves found themselves in Canada—and free at last.

In 1905, a group of militant Negroes had answered a call for "aggressive action" from W. E. B. Du Bois and W. M. Trotter. They met on the Canadian side of Niagara Falls.

Harpers Ferry was where John Brown and his band had laid down their lives to free the slaves. In this place, the Niagara men and women dedicated themselves "to the final emancipation of the race which John Brown died to make free." Among the marchers were relatives of men who had died with John Brown. They all sang "The Battle Hymn of the Republic": "John Brown's body lies amouldering in the grave . . . but his soul goes marching on."

The Niagara marchers declared in a statement, written by Du Bois:

". . . We will not be satisfied to take one jot or tittle less than our full manhood rights. We claim for ourselves every single right that belongs to a freeborn American, political, civil, and social; and until we get these rights we will never cease to protest and assail the ears of America."

The statement made this important point:

"The battle we wage is not for ourselves alone but for all true Americans. It is a fight for ideals, lest this, our common fatherland, false to its founding, become in truth the land of the thief and the home of the Slave . . ."

The demands of the Niagara Movement were:

"First, we would vote; with the right to vote goes everything . . .

"Second. We want discrimination in public accommodation to cease. Separation in railway and street cars, based simply on race and color, is un-American, undemocratic, and silly . . .

"Third. We claim the right of freemen to walk, talk, and be with them that wish to be with us . . .

"Fourth. We want the laws enforced against rich as well as poor; against Capitalist as well as Laborer; against white as well as black . . .

"Fifth. We want our children educated. The school system in the country districts of the South is a disgrace and in few towns and cities are the Negro schools what they ought to be.

". . . We want our children trained as intelligent human beings should be, and we will fight for all time against any proposal to educate black boys and girls simply as servants and underlings, or simply for the use of other people. They have a right to know, to think, to aspire . . ."

The men of Niagara hoped to achieve their demands by voting, by insisting on rights, and by hammering away at the truth. There was to be no violence, but they did dedicate themselves to the fighting spirit of John Brown.

The men and women of Niagara refused to give over the leadership of their race to "cowards and trucklers," they said. "We are men; we will be treated as men . . . We will never give up . . . And we shall win . . . Courage, brothers! The battle for humanity is not lost or losing. All across the skies sit signs of promise . . . Above are the everlasting stars."

These words, ringing with bravery and hope, to some people seemed foolish and idealistic—to others, revolutionary. Harpers Ferry was only the beginning of a long march.

How did W. E. B. Du Bois move out of his quiet study at Atlanta to the powerful public spotlight of Harpers Ferry?

He never gave up his fervent belief in learning. But his views shifted. At first he thought ignorance alone caused racial prejudice and that the "truth" of science and history could rid the world of prejudice. Du Bois was first and foremost a thinker. He had vowed in 1893 "to make a name in science, to make a name in literature and thus to raise my race . . ."

A brilliant student and a successful scholar, he believed that other talented young Negroes should have the opportunities he had. He called these youth "The Talented Tenth." From their ranks would come the militant leadership Negroes needed for the long march to freedom.

A letter Du Bois wrote to a Negro high school girl in Berwyn, Pennsylvania, in 1905, bears out his views.

"If you train yourself as you easily can, there are wonderful chances of usefulness before you; you can join the ranks of 15,000 Negro women teachers, of hundreds of nurses and physicians, of the growing number of clerks and stenographers, and above all the host of home-makers. Ignorance is a cure for nothing. Get the very best training possible and the doors of opportunity will fly open before you . . . On the other hand, every time a colored person neglects an opportunity, it makes it more difficult for others of the race to get such an opportunity. Do you want to cut off the chances of the boys and girls of tomorrow?"

At Harvard University, for his Doctor of Philosophy degree, he wrote *The Suppression of the African Slave Trade*. Published in 1896 it became the first volume of the Harvard Historical Studies.

At the University of Berlin, Germany, he became in-

Du Bois was first and foremost a scholar. He had vowed in 1893 "to make a name in science, to make a name in literature and thus to raise my race . . ."

terested in the new study of sociology. It was a way of studying people and how they lived together in society—their jobs, their homes, their religion, their politics, their recreation.

In Philadelphia, Du Bois first put the new sociology into practice. He made a study of Negroes living in that city for the University of Pennsylvania. The first scientific study of Negro life in the city, it was published in 1899 as *The Philadelphia Negro*.

In Atlanta, he studied the lives of Negroes in the South. He directed the Atlanta University studies—16 in all. They included: *The Negro in Business; Social and Physical Conditions of Negroes in Cities; Notes on Negro Crime; The Negro Artisan; The Negro Church; The Negro School*.

Dr. Du Bois was searching for—and finding—the truth about Negroes. His studies showed that Negroes were shaped by their past and present lives. In this they were no different from all men.

His scholarly findings were widely accepted and respected by thinkers around the world. But were they accepted by the people of America—government officials, businessmen, ordinary people on farms, and in shops and factories?

As far as Du Bois could see, this truth was having little effect on the beliefs of most white Americans or on the conditions of most black Americans. Du Bois watched the steady rise of Jim Crow. He experienced it himself in Atlanta, where he had to ride at the back of the streetcars. A scholar, he could not use the public library, though some of his own books were on the shelves. He was horrified when a Negro farmer he had known was lynched.

Du Bois was changing. He felt truth alone was not enough. What he saw no longer allowed him to be cool and reasonable. He began to write—and act—with greater passion. He could not stay calm as he watched the sufferings of his people.

He never gave up his studies and his writing. However, for the rest of his long life, he sought active ways to use his knowledge—ways to bring about changes more quickly.

Du Bois expressed with great feeling, the longings, the confusion, and the deep disappointments of the Negro in trying "to be both a Negro and an American." Black folk were haunted by poverty, lack of education, and prejudice.

Du Bois was sickened that black folk in America were taught to look down on everything black. This could be seen in the language itself. People talked about *black days, black sheep, blackguards, black markets.* They *blackballed, blackmailed,* and *blacklisted.* People gave *black looks* and got *black marks.*

Du Bois issued the call of Niagara. But Negroes alone could not fight the two separate worlds of race. They needed help to overcome Jim Crow.

Help came in a strange way. Between 1900 and 1910 there were six major riots in the U.S. Two were in the South and four in the North.

It is sad that it often takes the shock of a riot to remind white Americans that Negroes exist and object to their present burdens.

One such riot was in Springfield, Illinois, in 1908. It shocked liberal whites and moved them to hold out their hands to the Negroes of Niagara. They saw that the questions asked by men such as Dr. Penn of Atlanta had to be answered. Some white Americans began to realize that there must be only one America.

The time for action had come.

On February 12, 1909—the 100th anniversary of the birth of Abraham Lincoln—53 men and women issued a call for a meeting in New York City on the problems of the Negro. Oswald Garrison Villard, an editor and the grandson of William Lloyd Garrison the famous abolitionist and editor of *The Liberator,* wrote the call. He said, "This government cannot exist half-slave and half-free any better today than it could in 1861."

The conference was held from May 30 to June 1, 1909. Some whites feared that the Negroes would be too out-spoken and radical. If at all possible, they wanted to avoid an open break with Booker T. Washington. Washington, along with certain Negro leaders who disapproved of aggressive action, chose not to take part. They said things are bad, but Negroes should not agitate.

Other militant Negroes, such as William Monroe Trotter and Ida Baker Wells-Barnett, were distrustful. They feared the white liberals would take over the movement and water it down. They had little confidence in their newfound white allies.

Out of this meeting grew the National Association for the Advancement of Colored People (NAACP), the first of the modern civil rights organizations.

The NAACP was organized in 1910. Du Bois left

Atlanta University to become its Director of Publicity and Research. All its first officers, except Du Bois, were white. Eight Negroes did become members of the Board of Directors. Later others joined the front ranks. Moorfield Story, a Boston lawyer, was the first president.

The NAACP aimed to study the problems of race in the United States. It was going to seek a legal end to these wrongs. The NAACP tried to get new laws passed to protect Negroes. It sent its lawyers into courts to defend rights of Negroes already protected under the Constitution and existing laws.

Du Bois edited the NAACP's monthly magazine, *Crisis,* for 20 years. The first issue came out in November 1910 and was an immediate success. The number of subscribers jumped from 1000 to 31,000 in four years. Du Bois wrote in an early editorial:

"The great day is coming . . . We have crawled and pleaded for justice and we have been cheerfully spit upon and murdered and burned. We will not endure it forever. If we are to die, in God's name, let us perish like men and not like bales of hay."

Du Bois' view of the race problem went far beyond the borders of the United States. It has been said that he had a "world view of race." In Du Bois' time, such a view was rare.

Du Bois took part in early Pan-African Congresses. The first such meeting ever held was in London in 1900, attended by 32 representatives. Four were from Africa —two from British colonies, Sierra Leone and the Gold Coast (now Ghana), and two from independent nations, Ethiopia and Liberia. (The only other independent

Negro nation then was Haiti.) The other delegates came from the United States and the Caribbean islands.

It was at this meeting that Du Bois first spoke his famous prediction, "The problem of the twentieth century is the problem of the color line . . ." The meeting protested the treatment of Africans in South Africa and Rhodesia. Her Majesty's Government assured the delegates that it would not "overlook the interests and the welfare of the native races."

Du Bois summed up the accomplishments of the conference: "This meeting attracted attention (and) put the word 'Pan-African' in the dictionaries for the first time." This and later Congresses—six in all from 1900 to 1945—were the beginnings of the successful drive for African independence.

Du Bois, however, did not stop at the brotherhood of men of color. He hoped for the brotherhood of all men.

But in the U.S., brotherhood was a long way off. The long pull to freedom was slow and painful. In 1911, a second group formed the Urban League. Made up of Negroes and whites, it used quieter methods than did the NAACP. Working mostly with the streams of Negroes moving to Northern cities, the league helped them to adjust to city life, to find jobs and homes. Over the years, Urban League officials bargained with government officials and businessmen for better jobs, better homes, and better education for Negroes. Their motto: "Not Alms but Opportunity." Though the work of the two new groups overlapped, generally the NAACP tried to help the Negro through the courts; the Urban League through providing jobs and homes.

No results could be seen of these civil rights efforts for a number of years. The first big NAACP victory was in 1915. NAACP lawyers presented their case against "Grandfather Clauses" that let whites vote even though they lacked the same literacy, tax, and other qualifications for which Negroes were barred from voting. The Supreme Court declared them unconstitutional.

The march that started sixty years ago at Harpers Ferry has continued through the years. The marchers and the freedom-riders still seek the same goals—equal rights for all Americans in jobs, housing, voting, and education. It shall continue until the doors to first-class citizenship are opened for all Americans.

INDEX

Harlan, John Marshall, 78–79
Hayes, Rutherford B., President, 28, 30–31, 33
History of the Negro Race in America (book), 93
Home rule, restoration of, 24
Hope, John, 88, 103

Impeachment, Johnson's, 10–11
Imperialism, 47, 56–57
See also Colonialism
Independent, The (magazine), 96

Jim Crow, rise of, 58–67, 73–76
law for railroads, 74
Johnson, Andrew, President, 7
impeachment of, 10–11
plans for Reconstruction, 8–12
Johnson, James Weldon, 100

Ku Klux Klan, 46
"Dead Books," 19
formation of the, 19–22

Labor unions, forming of, 36
Lee, Robert E., General, 9
Lemmons, Bob, 39
Liberator, The (newspaper), 112
Lincoln, Abraham, President, 33, 74, 112
issues Emancipation Proclamation, 32
plans for Reconstruction, 5–7, 8
Lynch, John Roy, 15
Lynchings, 76

McKinley, William, President, 50, 55
Maine (battleship), 50
"Mississippi Pig Law," 35
Mix, Tom, 39

Nadir period in the United States, 91
Nash, Beverly, 14
Nation, The (magazine), 57
National Association for the Advancement of Colored People (NAACP), 112–15
National Negro Business League, 94
New Orleans *Times* (newspaper), 30
New Republic (magazine), 87
New York *Age* (newspaper), 93
New York *World* (newspaper), 80
Niagara Movement, 103, 106

Pan-African Congresses, 113
Paris Exhibition of 1897, 92
Penn, W. F., 95, 112
Philadelphia Negro, The (book), 110
Pickett, Bill, 39
Pinchback, P. B. S., 15
Plessy v. Ferguson (court battle), 78
Poll taxes, 69, 73
See also Voting, Negroes and
Populists (political party), 62–63, 67, 68
Prosperity of the South Dependent on the Elevation of the Negro, The (book), 61

Racism, 44–47
See also Jim Crow, rise of; Ku Klux Klan
Radical Reconstruction, 13, 17, 18, 19, 23, 30
See also Reconstruction
Railroads, Jim Crow law for, 74
Rainey, Joseph, 16
Rapier, James T., 24